The Limits of Restraint

The Military Implications of a Restrained U.S. Grand Strategy in the Asia-Pacific

MIRANDA PRIEBE, KRISTEN GUNNESS, KARL P. MUELLER, ZACHARY BURDETTE

T0308370

NATIONAL SECURITY RESEARCH DIVISION

For more information on this publication, visit **www.rand.org/t/RRA739-4**.

About RAND

The RAND Corporation is a research organization that develops solutions to public policy challenges to help make communities throughout the world safer and more secure, healthier and more prosperous. RAND is nonprofit, nonpartisan, and committed to the public interest. To learn more about RAND, visit www.rand.org.

Research Integrity

Our mission to help improve policy and decisionmaking through research and analysis is enabled through our core values of quality and objectivity and our unwavering commitment to the highest level of integrity and ethical behavior. To help ensure our research and analysis are rigorous, objective, and nonpartisan, we subject our research publications to a robust and exacting quality-assurance process; avoid both the appearance and reality of financial and other conflicts of interest through staff training, project screening, and a policy of mandatory disclosure; and pursue transparency in our research engagements through our commitment to the open publication of our research findings and recommendations, disclosure of the source of funding of published research, and policies to ensure intellectual independence. For more information, visit www.rand.org/about/principles.

RAND's publications do not necessarily reflect the opinions of its research clients and sponsors.

Published by the RAND Corporation, Santa Monica, Calif.
© 2022 RAND Corporation
RAND® is a registered trademark.

Library of Congress Cataloging-in-Publication Data is available for this publication.
ISBN: 978-1-9774-0890-7

Cover: U.S. Navy photo.

About This Report

In recent years, there has been growing interest in rethinking U.S. grand strategy, or the U.S. approach to the world. This report is the second in a series examining the policy implications of a realist grand strategy of restraint, a prominent alternative to the current U.S. approach. The purpose of the series is to help policymakers and the public better understand how U.S. policy would change under such a strategy and evaluate the trade-offs associated with this approach. The first report in this series, *Implementing Restraint: Changes in U.S. Regional Security Policies to Operationalize a Realist Grand Strategy of Restraint* (by Miranda Priebe, Bryan Rooney, Nathan Beauchamp-Mustafaga, Jeffrey Martini, and Stephanie Pezard, published in 2021, available at www.rand.org/t/RRA739-1), summarizes security policies that advocates of restraint have proposed for key regions and identifies areas in which more analysis is needed to develop the policy implications of restraint.

In this report, we focus on the Asia-Pacific, a portion of the larger region that the U.S. government refers to as the *Indo-Pacific*. This report describes when the United States would use force in the Asia-Pacific, proposes possible warfighting scenarios that would guide U.S. Department of Defense planning, and describes how U.S. posture in the Asia-Pacific region would change if the United States adopted a grand strategy of restraint.

In addition to discussing the implications of restraint, this report considers a series of scenarios involving the defense of Japan that have not been a focus of the defense policy community, along with implications for U.S. posture and capabilities. Therefore, this report may be of interest to policymakers, military planners, and analysts considering U.S. preparedness for conflict in the Indo-Pacific region over the long term.

RAND Center for Analysis of U.S. Grand Strategy

This research was conducted within the RAND Center for Analysis of U.S. Grand Strategy. The center's mission is to inform the debate about the U.S. role in the world by more clearly specifying new approaches to U.S. grand strategy, evaluating the logic of different approaches, and identifying the trade-offs that each option creates. Initial funding for the center was provided by a seed grant from the Charles Koch Institute, now called the Stand Together Trust. Ongoing funding comes from RAND Corporation supporters and from foundations and philanthropists.

The center is an initiative of the International Security and Defense Policy Center of the RAND National Security Research Division (NSRD). NSRD conducts research and analysis for the Office of the Secretary of Defense, the U.S. Intelligence Community, U.S. State Department, allied foreign governments, and foundations.

For more information on the RAND Center for Analysis of U.S. Grand Strategy, see www.rand.org/nsrd/isdp/grand-strategy or contact the center director (contact information is provided on the webpage).

Acknowledgments

We thank Nathan Beauchamp-Mustafaga, Cortez Cooper, Abby Doll, David Frelinger, Jacob Heim, Jeffrey Hornung, Bradley Martin, and Barry Wilson for participating in roundtables on the warfighting scenarios discussed in this report. We also thank Emma Ashford, Jasen Castillo, Eugene Gholz, Eric Gomez, and other advocates of restraint for taking the time to speak with us about their views. Finally, we thank Maggie Habib for research assistance.

Summary

Issue

Currently, there is bipartisan support for the Biden administration's approach toward China, which includes maintaining U.S. security leadership, strengthening U.S. alliances and partnerships, and increasing U.S. military forces in the Indo-Pacific region. In the years ahead, however, policymakers might wish to consider alternative approaches to China and the region and the trade-offs they would create. One of the most prominent alternatives is a grand strategy of restraint, an approach to the world that would define U.S. interests more narrowly, place a greater emphasis on diplomacy, reduce the size of the military and U.S. forward military presence, renegotiate or end U.S. security commitments, and raise the bar for the use of force. The community of those who support some or all of these policies has expanded beyond the scholars who originally developed the underlying logic of restraint. It now includes a growing number of foreign policy analysts, policymakers on both sides of the aisle, and veterans and anti-war grassroots groups. Previous RAND research identified unanswered questions about what this type of strategy would mean in practice for U.S. security policy in the Asia-Pacific region. For example, when would advocates of restraint support the use of force to defend U.S. interests, and what military posture would the United States need in the region to respond to threats in the next decade?

Approach

Fully answering these questions will require detailed analysis, as well as more-specific discussions among those who advocate a grand strategy of restraint. We provide a framework for structuring these next steps and conduct preliminary analysis to offer an initial set of answers. We draw on writings by and interviews with advocates of restraint and extend their logic to identify their key objectives for the Asia-Pacific region. We then assess the threat that China could pose to these objectives in the coming decade. Using this assessment, we identify missions that the U.S. military might be asked to prepare to execute under a grand strategy of restraint and propose three candidate warfighting scenarios that could guide U.S. Department of Defense planning under a strategy of restraint. These scenarios all involve a Chinese attack on Japan, a country that most restrainers would be willing to help defend given its wealth and geography. We used expert roundtables to develop an initial understanding of how the United States would need to prepare for these scenarios and to identify priorities for U.S. military posture in the region under a grand strategy of restraint.

Key Findings

Restrainers have a variety of views about when to use force in the Asia-Pacific. These views range from a narrow focus on the defense of the U.S. homeland to a more expansive U.S. role that includes the defense of Japan and South Korea. Restrainers generally do not support using force to defend Taiwan, to uphold other countries' claims to disputed maritime areas, or to maintain access to coastal waters on China's periphery.

Given their articulation of U.S. interests and our assessment of current threats, we assess that the defense of Japan would be the primary driver of U.S. posture in the Asia-Pacific for most restrainers. Other factors that would influence U.S. posture include restrainers' preferences for a smaller military force structure, fewer forward-deployed forces, and wartime operating approaches that minimize attacks on the Chinese homeland. Our findings about the defense of Japan under a grand strategy of restraint are as follows:

- Defending Japan against a major Chinese attack would likely require maintaining some forward-deployed U.S. naval forces and pre-positioned materiel in the Asia-Pacific.
- Restrainers might be able to achieve their limited objective of helping Japan maintain its independence and defending the Ryukyu Islands from a Chinese attack and still reduce forward-deployed ground and, possibly, land-based air forces as they prefer.
- Restrainers would need to prioritize strategic airlift and sealift to deploy air and naval forces quickly and in large numbers from the United States.
- Given China's ability to target bases and ports, the United States would still need access to a large number of wartime operating locations in partner countries to increase the survivability of its forces involved in the defense of Japan.
- To have the capability to impose a distant blockade on China in response to an attack on Japan, the United States would need to maintain a large navy.
- In designing an appropriate posture, restrainers would face the same trade-offs between maximizing U.S. preparedness for conflict and incentivizing Japanese burden-sharing that policymakers currently confront.

Recommendations

We draw on restrainers' existing writing and extend their logic to describe the military implications of restraint as currently formulated. As restrainers with varying perspectives continue to refine their recommendations and discuss differences of threat assessment and prescription within the restraint community, we recommend that they be explicit about the conditions under which they would favor the use of force by the United States. We also recommend additional analysis to validate and refine our preliminary findings about U.S. posture under a grand strategy of restraint. Particularly, we recommend that advocates of restraint and military analysts use wargames, modeling, and other research methods to do the following:

- Assess Japan's ability to defend its coasts and airspace against a major Chinese attack. This would inform how much and what types of support the United States needs to provide to preserve Japan as an independent power, which many restrainers consider a vital objective.
- Calculate force and logistics requirements and timelines for deploying U.S. air and maritime forces to and within the Asia-Pacific. Many restrainers prefer to keep forces in the United States during peacetime, but more-detailed analysis is necessary to assess where the United States would need to station its forces in peacetime to achieve restrainers' wartime objectives related to the defense of Japan.
- Evaluate the implications of emerging technologies for a restraint-oriented posture in the Asia-Pacific. Technological advances may change the regional balance of power, options for how China could attack, and how Japan and the United States could defend against such aggression. Restrainers should address the implications of these technologies when making recommendations about force posture and wartime operational approaches.

Contents

Figures and Tables

Figures

Tables

CHAPTER ONE

Introduction

There has been growing bipartisan support in the United States for a confrontational strategy toward China. The Trump administration's 2017 National Security Strategy and 2018 National Defense Strategy emphasized the U.S. focus on great-power competition.[1] Similarly, the Biden administration's approach toward China has prioritized expanding and strengthening U.S. alliances and partnerships, increasing U.S. military forces in the Indo-Pacific region, and confronting China over its economic and security policies.[2] Although this approach currently has bipartisan support, China is a long-term security challenge, and policymakers and the public in the years ahead may wish to consider a wider variety of options for U.S. strategy in the region. This report considers one of the most prominent alternatives: the regional vision put forward by advocates of a realist grand strategy of restraint.[3] Globally, these strategists would define U.S. interests more narrowly, place a greater emphasis on diplomacy, reduce the size of the military and U.S. forward military presence, renegotiate or end some U.S. security commitments, and raise the bar for the use of force. Advocates of restraint have described their strategy in broad terms and offered some specific policy implications,

---

[1] White House, *National Security Strategy of the United States of America*, Washington, D.C., December 2017; Jim Mattis, *Summary of the 2018 National Defense Strategy of the United States of America*, Washington, D.C.: Department of Defense, 2018.

[2] For the Biden administration's approach, see Derek Grossman, "Biden's Indo-Pacific Policy Blueprint Emerges," Nikkei Asia, August 23, 2021; and White House, *Interim National Security Strategic Guidance*, Washington, D.C., March 2021. For discussion of the Trump administration's approach, see U.S. Department of Defense, *Indo-Pacific Strategy Report: Preparedness, Partnerships, and Promoting a Networked Region*, Arlington, Va., June 1, 2019; National Security Council, "U.S. Strategic Framework for the Indo-Pacific," Washington, D.C., February 2018; and U.S. Department of State, *A Free and Open Indo-Pacific: Advancing a Shared Vision*, Washington, D.C., November 4, 2019.

[3] We define *grand strategy* as "a state's logic for how it will use all of its instruments of national power to defend and promote its vital interests given international and domestic constraints" (Miranda Priebe, Bryan Rooney, Nathan Beauchamp-Mustafaga, Jeffrey Martini, and Stephanie Pezard, *Implementing Restraint: Changes in U.S. Regional Security Policies to Operationalize a Realist Grand Strategy of Restraint*, Santa Monica, Calif.: RAND Corporation, RR-A739-1, 2021, p. 1). For examples of recent calls for the United States to adopt a grand strategy of restraint, see Emma Ashford, "Strategies of Restraint: Remaking America's Broken Foreign Policy," *Foreign Affairs*, Vol. 100, No. 5, September–October 2021; Benjamin H. Friedman, *Restraint: A Post-COVID-19 U.S. National Security Strategy*, Washington, D.C.: Defense Priorities, 2020; and Brandon Valeriano and Eric Gomez, "Foreign Policy Restraint: A Bold Idea for Biden's First 100 Days," *American Conservative*, January 29, 2021.

but they have not yet fully developed many other details about what such a strategy would look like in practice.[4] To help U.S. policymakers and the public understand what advocates of restraint recommend and evaluate the trade-offs associated with their proposals, we take initial steps toward developing some of those details. In particular, we focus on the strategy's implications for the military dimensions of U.S. policy in the Asia-Pacific region.[5] The U.S. Department of Defense (DoD) currently organizes its planning around the region it calls the *Indo-Pacific*, which includes South Asia and extends across most of the Northern and Southern Pacific Oceans. We use the term *Asia-Pacific* in this report because we are focusing more specifically on the area from Southeast Asia across the northern and central Pacific Ocean to the U.S. West Coast, in which the greatest potential for conflict between China and the United States appears to lie.

The military implications of any given strategy depend largely on wartime considerations. Although advocates of restraint often focus on wars that they do not want the United States to fight, such as interventions in the Middle East, they are not isolationists who oppose U.S. military involvement abroad in all circumstances. Their list of vital interests worth fighting for is shorter than has been common for the United States in recent decades, but these strategists advocate maintaining substantial, although smaller, military forces. Of course, wartime considerations are not the only determinant of the military implications of a strategy. Advocates of restraint are often particularly attentive to the ways in which peacetime posture and military activities can affect the behavior of adversaries and allies, the likelihood of war, and the long-term sustainability of a strategy. Therefore, the military implications of restraint also flow from this broader set of considerations.

We offer a framework for moving from a broad vision for restraint to addressing more of the practical details that would guide defense officials if the United States adopted such a strategy. To analyze the military implications of a grand strategy of restraint in the Asia-Pacific in greater detail, we ask the following questions:

- What are the principles that restrainers believe should guide peacetime military posture and activities, as well as the way the United States should fight?
- What are the strategy's objectives for the Asia-Pacific region?
- What are the potential threats to those objectives in the next decade?
- Given these threats, what military missions would DoD need to be prepared to execute under a grand strategy of restraint?
- What warfighting scenarios would guide DoD planning?
- What capabilities would the United States need to prevail in these scenarios?
- What are the broad implications for U.S. military posture in the Asia-Pacific?

---

[4] For a summary of the policy prescriptions that restrainers put forward by region, see Priebe et al., 2021.

[5] For a map of U.S. Indo-Pacific Command's area of responsibility, see U.S. Indo-Pacific Command, "USINDOPACOM Area of Responsibility," webpage, undated b.

In Chapter Two of this report, we describe the objectives that restrainers might seek in the Asia-Pacific, assess threats to those objectives, and identify the military missions and scenarios that might drive DoD planning under a grand strategy of restraint. In Chapters Three through Five, we analyze three candidate defense planning scenarios by describing U.S., allied, and Chinese strategies and identifying, in broad terms, the posture that the United States would need to prevail in such a scenario. Chapter Six concludes with our findings and recommendations for future analysis.

Debates within the restraint community about the Asia-Pacific region are ongoing. Our intent is to provide policymakers with our best understanding of how advocates of restraint would answer these questions given the current state of that discussion. We hope the framework that we develop in this report will also inform continued analysis of this topic and advance future debates about it.

Overview of a Grand Strategy of Restraint

Since World War II, U.S. grand strategy has revolved around a vast system of alliances and partnerships, a large forward military presence, and frequent military interventions. Although there have been variations across administrations, the United States has generally conceived of its interests broadly, seeing stability in key regions, especially Europe, Asia, and the Middle East, as a vital U.S. interest. Conversely, advocates of restraint, or *restrainers*, have argued that this approach has undermined U.S. security by increasing tensions with other states, such as Russia and China, disincentivizing allies from preparing for their own defense, and involving the United States in costly and unnecessary wars. Moreover, these strategists contend that the key elements of U.S. grand strategy since the end of the Cold War are increasingly unsustainable as other countries become stronger and as the United States faces challenges at home.[6]

For many years, advocates of a more restrained approach to U.S. grand strategy were primarily in academia or at the libertarian CATO Institute.[7] There has not been a systematic assessment of the size or influence of this community today. However, there are several indicators that suggest that the ideas put forward by restrainers are becoming more influential

---

[6] John J. Mearsheimer, *The Great Delusion: Liberal Dreams and International Realities*, New Haven, Conn.: Yale University Press, 2018; John J. Mearsheimer and Stephen M. Walt, "The Case for Offshore Balancing: A Superior U.S. Grand Strategy," *Foreign Affairs*, Vol. 95, No. 4, July–August 2016; Barry R. Posen, *Restraint: A New Foundation for U.S. Grand Strategy*, Ithaca, N.Y.: Cornell University Press, 2014; Stephen M. Walt, *The Hell of Good Intentions: America's Foreign Policy Elite and the Decline of U.S. Primacy*, New York: Farrar, Straus and Giroux, 2018a. As we discuss later, Walt and Mearsheimer share many assumptions and policy prescriptions with other restrainers but diverge significantly on U.S. strategy in Asia.

[7] See, for example, Eugene Gholz, Daryl G. Press, and Harvey M. Sapolsky, "Come Home, America: The Strategy of Restraint in the Face of Temptation," *International Security*, Vol. 21, No. 4, Spring 1997; Christopher Layne, "From Preponderance to Offshore Balancing: America's Future Grand Strategy," *International Security*, Vol. 22, No. 1, Summer 1997; Mearsheimer and Walt, 2016; and Posen, 2014.

even though restraint remains a minority position. For example, these voices are featured in mainstream media outlets and foreign policy establishments.[8] Those who oppose restraint have spoken out against the community's perceived influence in the national conversation.[9] Some key themes of restraint have filtered into the platforms of prominent politicians, such as Bernie Sanders's and Elizabeth Warren's calls to end endless wars and Donald Trump's focus on allied free-riding and withdrawal from Afghanistan (even as he pursued other policies that restrainers opposed).[10] These examples illustrate how the restraint community crosses traditional partisan divides. It includes libertarians concerned that activism abroad harms liberty at home, budget hawks worried about the sustainability of the defense budget for fiscal reasons, progressive democrats who want to use national security funds on their domestic priorities, and veterans and anti-war groups skeptical of U.S. interventions abroad.[11] This report acknowledges the wide variety of views within the broader restraint community. The discussions that follow, however, focus on the longest-standing and most fully articulated versions of restraint that originate primarily from realist scholars of international relations.[12]

Restrainers have a narrow conception of the interests that are vital, or important enough to be worth defending with U.S. military force. This list includes protecting the populace, sovereignty, and territorial integrity of the United States.[13] Restrainers also prioritize retain-

---

[8] See, for example, restraint voices (e.g., Emma Ashford, Stephen Wertheim, Stephen Walt) in the following articles and commentaries: "Is U.S. Foreign Policy Too Hostile to China? *Foreign Affairs* Asks the Experts," *Foreign Affairs*, October 19, 2021; Will Ruger, "To Defend America, Don't Overreach," *New York Times*, March 19, 2018; and Bret Stephens, Emma Ashford, and Stephen Sestanovich, "The Biden-Putin Summit: 'This Is Not About Trust,'" *New York Times*, June 16, 2021. Restraint-oriented analysts are now on staff at such organizations as the Atlantic Council and the Carnegie Endowment for International Peace (Scowcroft Center for Strategy and Security, "New American Engagement Initiative," webpage, Atlantic Council, undated). Other organizations are analyzing the implications of the restraint position without promoting it; see, for example, Kathleen H. Hicks and Joseph P. Federici, *Getting to Less? Exploring the Press for Less in America's Defense Commitments*, Washington, D.C.: Center for Strategic and International Studies, CSIS Briefs, January 2020; and Priebe et al., 2021.

[9] See, for example, Daniel Deudney and G. John Ikenberry, "Misplaced Restraint: The Quincy Coalition Versus Liberal Internationalism," *Survival*, Vol. 63, No. 4, August–September 2021; and Thomas Wright, "The Case Against Restraint," interview with Elliot Waldman, *World Politics Review*, podcast, June 2, 2021.

[10] Bernie Sanders, "Ending America's Endless War: We Must Stop Giving Terrorists Exactly What They Want," *Foreign Affairs*, June 24, 2019; Elizabeth Warren, "We Can End Our Endless Wars," *The Atlantic*, January 27, 2020; Eileen Sullivan, "Trump Questions the Core of NATO: Mutual Defense, Including Montenegro," *New York Times*, July 18, 2018.

[11] For example, the transpartisan Quincy Institute, which advocates a grand strategy of restraint, was formed with funding from sources as diverse as the Charles Koch Institute and the Open Society Foundations (see Quincy Institute for Responsible Statecraft, "About QI," webpage, undated).

[12] Ashford, 2021, pp. 132–134.

[13] Gholz, Press, and Sapolsky, 1997, p. 8; Christopher Layne, *The Peace of Illusions: American Grand Strategy from 1940 to the Present*, Ithaca, N.Y.: Cornell University Press, 2006, p. 160; Mearsheimer and Walt, 2016, pp. 72–73; Posen, 2014, pp. 3, 69–71.

ing sufficient military and economic power to do so over the long term.[14] Some restrainers also consider U.S. economic prosperity more generally to be a vital interest.[15] This conception of vital interests does not include spreading liberal values, such as democracy and human rights; demonstrating the strength of the United States or its willingness to fight; or promoting peace and stability abroad. Restrainers emphasize the principle that alliances are a means of protecting U.S. interests rather than an intrinsically valuable objective worth maintaining or fighting for in its own right.

Restrainers argue that less military engagement abroad would better serve U.S. interests. This would entail a reduced forward military presence, fewer or more-conditional security commitments, and a higher bar for the use of force. In addition to holding a narrower conception of what is worth fighting for, these strategists are skeptical that the threats to U.S. interests are as severe as many policymakers assess; argue that military solutions are usually unnecessary or even counterproductive in addressing the problems that the United States faces; and place a high priority on avoiding great-power wars because of the costs and potential risks, including nuclear escalation.[16] Under a grand strategy of restraint, the United States would rely more on diplomacy to manage conflicts of interest with potential adversaries and would encourage allies to assume the principal burden of defending themselves.

The restrainers on whom we focus in this report ground most of their arguments in the realist tradition of international relations theory, which begins from the premise that the absence of a central authority to enforce international agreements compels states to take measures to protect themselves.[17] Realists expect that states tend to balance against perceived threats when they must but will also free-ride on allies when they can. Restrainers therefore argue that U.S. allies and partners would do more to check potential aggressors, such as China and Russia, if the United States were to do less to guarantee those allies' protection.[18] Restrainers also worry that alliances can entangle the United States in war, so they seek to limit security commitments to those that are critical to U.S. security.[19] Restrainers assess that, by historical standards, the United States itself is extremely safe from military threats

---

[14] Posen, 2014, p. 1.

[15] Gholz, Press, and Sapolsky, 1997, pp. 5, 9.

[16] Emma Ashford, interview with the authors, video call, August 25, 2021; Eric Gomez, interview with the authors, video call, August 20, 2021; Posen, 2014. Although Glaser does not self-identify as a restrainer, his views overlap in some areas with the views of the restraint community, including on the risks of great-power conflict (Charles L. Glaser, "A U.S.-China Grand Bargain? The Hard Choice Between Military Competition and Accommodation," *International Security*, Vol. 39, No. 4, Spring 2015).

[17] Kenneth N. Waltz, *Theory of International Politics*, Reading, Mass.: Addison-Wesley Publishing Company, Inc., 1979.

[18] Posen, 2014, pp. 71–91; Stephen M. Walt, *The Origins of Alliances*, Ithaca, N.Y.: Cornell University Press, 1987.

[19] A. Trevor Thrall and Benjamin H. Friedman, "National Interests, Grand Strategy, and the Case for Restraint," in A. Trevor Thrall and Benjamin H. Friedman, eds., *US Grand Strategy in the 21st Century: The Case for Restraint*, New York: Routledge, 2018.

because of its military strength, nuclear arsenal, and geographic location far from other powerful states.

Although restraint advocates tend to hold a number of foundational beliefs in common, there are some significant differences within the camp. Most consequentially, restrainers generally agree that current policy overstates the threat that China poses to the United States but nevertheless vary in their assessments of how much lower and how remote the threat is. Restrainers also disagree about the relative importance of various reasons for retrenchment, including encouraging allies to provide for their own defense,[20] limiting spirals of hostility and avoidable wars with powerful adversaries,[21] avoiding tempting U.S. leaders to embark on imprudent military adventures,[22] and reducing the defense budget.[23]

There are different varieties of restraint, which we group into three archetypal categories. Many theorists do not fit neatly into a single group, and few use these terms to describe themselves, but some of the disagreements among restrainers are significant enough that it is analytically important to distinguish among different camps. The first variant, which we call *defensive restraint*, focuses narrowly on defending the homeland and U.S. territories. Restrainers in this camp assess that there are few direct threats to the security of the United States today and that the United States can address more-serious future threats if and when they arise. In the meantime, the United States can afford to rely primarily on its secure geographical position and nuclear deterrence rather than maintaining large military forces and stationing them abroad. Strategists in this camp are skeptical that preventing China from dominating its region or interfering with trade in the Pacific are essential to U.S. security. As a result, these restrainers call for global retrenchment that would entail ending many U.S. alliances and security relationships, dramatically curtailing overseas military presence, and substantially reducing overall military force structure.[24]

---

[20] Jasen J. Castillo, interview with the authors, video call, May 3, 2021.

[21] Eugene Gholz, interview with the authors, video call, April 30, 2021.

[22] John Mueller, *The Stupidity of War: American Foreign Policy and the Case for Complacency*, Cambridge, United Kingdom: Cambridge University Press, 2021, pp. 197–199.

[23] For a more detailed discussion of restrainers' views on the economic effects of the defense budget and evidence from the economics literature, see Bryan Rooney, Grant Johnson, and Miranda Priebe, *How Does Defense Spending Affect Economic Growth?* Santa Monica, Calif.: RAND Corporation, RR-A739-2, 2021. See Posen, 2014, for a view that the size of the defense budget is one of many factors that justifies restraint. For an example that is chiefly concerned with the defense budget, see Doug Bandow, "Now's the Time to Become a Truly 'America First' Military," *American Conservative*, March 26, 2020.

[24] Eugene Gholz, interview with the authors, video call, April 30, 2021; Gholz, Press, and Sapolsky, 1997. In our last report in this series, we referred to this group as *advocates of minimal military involvement* (Priebe et al., 2021, pp. 49–82). This group does not self-identify as isolationists, because they follow a logic that allows the possibility that a greater threat to the United States could require greater military involvement abroad in the long term. However, in the current context, in which this group sees very low threats to the U.S. homeland, its policy prescriptions regarding military intervention arguably overlap to a large degree with those of isolationism.

Flexible restraint is more inclined to maintain the U.S. ability to intervene militarily to protect a somewhat wider range of U.S. interests and to provide an insurance policy in case the threat environment becomes more severe. Compared with defensive restrainers, these strategists argue that China's growing power and influence in its region could become a significant threat to U.S. vital interests sooner or with less warning. If China were able to dominate the Asia-Pacific region, it might be able to project power more easily against the U.S. homeland and North America in the future. However, flexible restrainers still see a lower threat to vital U.S. interests than many current U.S. policymakers do, and they argue that fewer interests warrant military intervention even if threats to those interests worsen. As a result, flexible restrainers call for a smaller U.S. forward military presence than exists today but are more cautious than defensive restrainers about how much to retrench from Asia.[25]

Finally, *counterhegemonic restraint* shares many principles with the other schools of thought, but it places greater emphasis on preventing China from dominating the Asia-Pacific, a possibility that its advocates consider to be less remote and more dangerous than defensive or flexible restrainers say. As a result, counterhegemonic restrainers are willing to maintain more alliances and a larger forward military presence in Asia to counter the growth of China's power.[26] They are also more inclined than other restrainers to consider military intervention in response to aggressive Chinese actions that could enhance China's military power if unchecked. However, they still have a smaller list of issues over which they would fight than recent U.S. administrations do, as we discuss below.

There is also a group of restrainers who call for retrenchment from other parts of the world, especially Europe and the Middle East, to shift resources to support existing U.S. commitments in Asia. These strategists make many of the same arguments about allied burden-sharing, entanglement, and minimal threats to U.S. interests when it comes to Europe and the Middle East. However, they differ in their assessments of U.S. interests in Asia and the threats that China poses to those interests. Most notably, they want to preserve the status quo in the region, including Taiwan's independence from China, whereas other restrainers see U.S. regional interests more narrowly.[27] Because these strategists largely share the same objectives as current U.S. Asia-Pacific strategy, their prescriptions are not a focus of this report.

On a spectrum of interventionism, restraint occupies a space between isolationist and hegemonic grand strategies (Figure 1.1). There are few true isolationist voices in the U.S. debate over U.S. grand strategy. In theory, an isolationist grand strategy would end U.S. mili-

---

[25] Posen, 2014, p. 91.

[26] Jasen J. Castillo, interview with the authors, video call, May 3, 2021.

[27] Advocate of restraint B, interview with the authors, video call, May 14, 2021; Mearsheimer and Walt, 2016. There are also some commentators who do not self-identify as restrainers who similarly call for U.S. retrenchment from other regions in order to shift limited resources to Asia (Elbridge Colby, "Don't Let Iran Distract from China," *Wall Street Journal*, September 24, 2019; Elbridge Colby, *The Strategy of Denial: American Defense in an Age of Great Power Conflict*, New Haven, Conn.: Yale University Press, 2021, pp. 72–74).

FIGURE 1.1

Alternative Grand Strategies

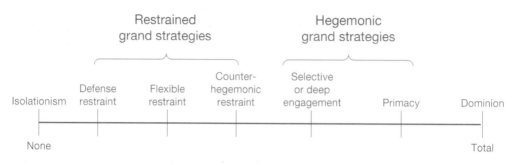

SOURCE: Adapted from Priebe et al., 2021.

tary involvement in international affairs.[28] Advocates of hegemonic grand strategies, in contrast, tend to view threats to U.S. interests as more immediate and severe than restrainers do, and they tend to emphasize the security and economic benefits of U.S. military superiority, forward military presence, and alliance commitments.[29] As with the restraint community, there are a variety of views within this camp about when and how to use force to advance U.S. interests.[30]

Advocates of restraint take clear stances regarding the types of wars that the United States should avoid fighting.[31] The restraint community has argued in particular against fighting wars to impose or defend democracy and to prevent nuclear proliferation. Some of the most vocal opponents of the 2003 invasion of Iraq were restrainers, as were those who criticized the expansion of U.S. aims in Afghanistan after the 2001 defeat of the Taliban regime. Restrainers believe that the U.S. withdrawal from Afghanistan was a correct and long overdue strategic choice, even if they believe that the Trump and Biden administrations mishandled its

---

[28] Bear Braumoeller, "The Myth of American Isolationism," *Foreign Policy Analysis*, Vol. 6, No. 4, October 2010. On the history of isolationism in the United States, see Charles A. Kupchan, *Isolationism: A History of America's Efforts to Shield Itself from the World*, New York: Oxford University Press, 2020.

[29] Stephen G. Brooks, G. John Ikenberry, and William C. Wohlforth, "Don't Come Home, America: The Case Against Retrenchment," *International Security*, Vol. 37, No. 3, Winter 2012–2013; Stephen G. Brooks and William C. Wohlforth, *America Abroad: Why the Sole Superpower Should Not Pull Back from the World*, New York: Oxford University Press, 2018.

[30] For example, Brooks and Wohlforth, 2018, draws a distinction between the authors' proposed strategy of "deep engagement" and "deep engagement plus," which would use force in a wider variety of circumstances, including to spread democracy.

[31] Priebe et al., 2021, pp. 134–135.

implementation.[32] However, while restrainers have consistently called for the United States to end what they term *endless wars* in the Middle East and South Asia, they have been vague about what threats *would* warrant a U.S. military response.[33] As a result, exactly how the military dimensions of U.S. policy in the Asia-Pacific would change if the United States adopted a grand strategy of restraint remains unclear.[34]

Principles That Would Guide U.S. Military Strategy Under a Grand Strategy of Restraint

Advocates of restraint offer several principles to guide U.S. peacetime military activities and posture, as well as how the United States should fight if it goes to war.

The United States should reduce reliance on military tools and the use of force. Advocates of restraint believe that the United States has an overmilitarized approach to the world and often uses force to defend or advance less-than-vital interests. Restrainers argue that there are many objectives and concerns that the United States should pursue with diplomatic or economic tools instead.[35] Because they believe that decisionmakers often underestimate the costs of war when considering the use of force, advocates of restraint call for careful assessments about what is actually worth defending.[36] When the United States is defending important but not vital interests, restrainers prefer alternatives to using force or, at most, fighting for limited military objectives in ways that limit costs and escalation risks.[37]

The United States should retain relative strength but not pursue global dominance. In recent years, U.S. policymakers have used such terms as *overmatch* to describe the high level of military advantage that they want to have over adversaries.[38] Advocates of restraint also prefer that the United States remain militarily stronger than other countries as a deterrent to attacks against vital U.S. interests.[39] However, unlike advocates of overmatch, they do not think that the United States should pursue military superiority where geographic or technological conditions are highly unfavorable, especially on the periphery of other great powers,

---

[32] Charles Koch Institute, "The Charles Koch Institute's Will Ruger on Status of U.S. Troop Withdrawal from Afghanistan," July 8, 2021; Stephen M. Walt, "Afghanistan Hasn't Damaged U.S. Credibility," *Foreign Policy*, August 21, 2021.

[33] Priebe et al., 2021.

[34] Posen has offered the most-detailed proposals on posture, but these were only intended to be rough estimates and were not based on a detailed analysis or specific warfighting scenarios (Posen, 2014, pp. 152–159).

[35] Gholz, Press, and Sapolsky, 1997, p. 10.

[36] Posen, 2014, pp. 22–23.

[37] Advocate of restraint A, interview with the authors, video call, May 6, 2021.

[38] White House, 2017, p. 28.

[39] Posen, 2014.

such as China.[40] Restrainers also believe that the pursuit of U.S. dominance can cause spirals of hostility that make conflict more likely. Moreover, they assess that seeking global dominance is not sustainable as the world becomes increasingly multipolar.

Allies should take the lead. In general, restrainers prefer that U.S. allies and partners take the lead in defending themselves. They argue that the United States has incurred high human and financial costs to provide security for others relative to what its own interests justify. As China in particular grows stronger, some advocates of restraint want allies to do more to strengthen a U.S.-supported counterbalancing coalition, and they worry that foreign partners will underinvest in their own defense if they can depend on U.S. protection. Finally, some restrainers point to the insecurity that U.S. security leadership provokes in such countries as China, Iran, and Russia. They argue that it is more threatening when a great power like the United States has forces on another state's periphery than when smaller powers build up their own defenses.[41] Among advocates of restraint, there are different perspectives about whether allied leadership means that the United States would only intervene to tip the balance in a war once it is underway or whether the United States should be ready to defeat aggression from the outset.[42]

The extent of an ally's preparations for its own defense might even determine whether some advocates of restraint would recommend supporting it in a crisis. If an ally or partner does little to address its vulnerabilities to China's growing power, then it will be more difficult to defend. The costs of protecting such states might therefore be higher than restrainers are willing to bear.[43]

The United States should limit onshore U.S. military presence in peacetime. Advocates of restraint are open to maintaining peacetime forward military presence when it is necessary to contain a significant threat, but, all else being equal, they prefer surging forces forward from the United States when the need arises. They tend to believe that geography gives

---

[40] Eugene Gholz, Benjamin H. Friedman, and Enea Gjoza, "Defensive Defense: A Better Way to Protect US Allies in Asia," *Washington Quarterly*, Vol. 42, No. 4, Winter 2020; Eugene Gholz, interview with the authors, video call, April 30, 2021; Barry R. Posen, "Command of the Commons: The Military Foundation of U.S. Hegemony," *International Security*, Vol. 28, No. 1, Summer 2003.

[41] Advocate of restraint A, interview with the authors, video call, May 6, 2021; Jasen J. Castillo, interview with the authors, video call, May 3, 2021; Layne, 2006, p. 169; Stephen M. Walt, "U.S. Grand Strategy After the Cold War: Can Realism Explain It? Should Realism Guide It?" *International Relations*, Vol. 32, No. 1, March 1, 2018b, p. 14. At least one advocate of restraint has argued that smaller states taking the lead in balancing might help regional aggressors recognize that it is their behavior rather than U.S. pressure that is provoking hostility among their neighbors (Advocate of restraint A, interview with the authors, video call, May 6, 2021).

[42] Castillo discusses these alternative views (Jasen J. Castillo, "Passing the Torch: Criteria for Implementing a Grand Strategy of Offshore Balancing," in Richard Fontaine and Loren DeJonge Schulman, eds., *New Voices in Grand Strategy*, Washington, D.C.: Center for a New American Security, 2019). We also heard these differences in our interviews (Jasen J. Castillo, interview with the authors, video call, May 3, 2021; Eugene Gholz, interview with authors, April 30, 2021).

[43] Advocate of restraint A, interview with the authors, video call, May 6, 2021.

the United States time to respond to threats before they become severe and, therefore, the risks of taking more time to flow forces to a conflict zone are often acceptable.[44]

Restrainers prefer to limit forward-deployed ground forces and land-based airpower and to rely instead on naval or long-range air forces operating from bases in U.S. territory.[45] A smaller presence in ally and partner countries, they contend, will incentivize these states to do more for their own defense. If fewer U.S. forces are deployed forward in peacetime, using force will also be more difficult, so U.S. leaders will face fewer temptations to intervene imprudently. Moreover, a smaller U.S. forward presence could reduce the risk of conflict by ameliorating security dilemmas with potential adversaries, which could make confrontations less likely, while U.S. forces being more remote could reduce both incentives and opportunities for preemptive attacks against them during a crisis. Finally, these strategists contend that, in some regions, U.S. forces provoke ill will among local populations, leading to anti-American sentiment and, in the extreme, terrorism.[46]

Advocates of restraint reject the claim that the United States needs to maintain a large peacetime presence overseas to make U.S. commitments credible to potential adversaries. They argue that the United States should only make commitments to use force when its vital interests are at stake. In these cases, restrainers contend, U.S. interests are "obvious to all" and, therefore, the presence of forward-deployed U.S. military forces is an unnecessary additional signal of U.S. interests.[47] Restrainers do not explain why U.S. interests should be obvious to other countries, but they presumably assume that such factors as geography, alliances, and economic ties are stronger predictors of U.S. strategic behavior than military presence. Restrainers note that communicating a U.S. willingness to fight over a peripheral interest can be more difficult, but they oppose fighting over less-than-vital interests anyway.

Although restrainers are conscious of the expense of U.S. defense policies and seek to reduce it, budgetary considerations are not the chief driver of restrainers' preference for minimizing onshore presence. Advocates of restraint acknowledge that some allies, including

---

[44] Patrick Porter, "The Tyrannies of Distance: Maritime Asia and the Barriers to Conquest," in A. Trevor Thrall and Benjamin H. Friedman, eds., *US Grand Strategy in the 21st Century: The Case for Restraint*, New York: Routledge, 2018.

[45] Jasen J. Castillo, interview with the authors, video call, May 3, 2021; Layne, 1997; Mearsheimer and Walt, 2016.

[46] Posen, 2014, p. 53; Walt, 2018a, p. 264. This argument is usually proffered about the effects of U.S. military presence in the Middle East, which does not necessarily apply directly to Asia and Europe, but U.S. presence in such locations as the Philippines and Japan has provoked local animosity.

[47] Stephen M. Walt, "The Credibility Addiction," *Foreign Policy*, January 6, 2015. Restrainers often cite Press in making their arguments about credibility (Daryl G. Press, *Calculating Credibility: How Leaders Assess Military Threats*, Ithaca, N.Y.: Cornell University Press, 2005). Restrainers' view on extended nuclear deterrence is somewhat different from their view about conventional forces. They argue that convincing an adversary that the United States would risk nuclear war over another country is more difficult and that the United States has historically adopted costly and risky policies (e.g., placing nuclear forces on an ally's soil) to do so. Therefore, restrainers contend that the United States should not take on such costs and risks for any but the most vital interests (Posen, 2014, p. 76).

Japan and South Korea, share some of the cost of forward-deployed U.S. forces. Restrainers recognize that the size of the U.S. armed forces, rather than where they are located, is the primary determinant of their cost.[48]

The U.S. military should prioritize defensive preparations and operational approaches. Advocates of restraint tend to worry about the possibility of spirals of hostility in peacetime and escalation in wartime.[49] To mitigate these risks, they recommend emphasizing defensive systems and operational approaches over offensive ones to the extent possible. In particular, restrainers tend to advocate that the United States and its allies invest in weapon systems that are most useful for defensive operations to deny states the ability to project power, such as anti-ship missiles and air defenses, rather than more-offensive capabilities that contribute to a potential adversary's fears of attack by the United States, such as long-range land-attack missiles, stealth bombers, and forward-deployed armored forces, although they acknowledge that distinguishing between offensive and defensive systems is often problematic.[50] Similarly, they prefer strategies and operational approaches that minimize or avoid strikes against the homeland of another great power because such attacks increase the risk of escalation, including the use of nuclear weapons.

Methodological Approach

In this report, we evaluate the military implications of restraint for the Asia-Pacific. We start with restrainers' writings to identify their key objectives in the region. We supplemented our review of the literature by interviewing six strategists who represent different positions within the restraint community.[51] We then consider information on China's capabilities and interests to assess potential threats to likely U.S. objectives under a grand strategy of restraint. Where plausible threats to restrainers' objectives exist in the coming decade, we propose mis-

---

[48] Posen, 2014, p. 41. Despite ally and partner contributions, basing overseas is generally more expensive than basing in the United States, although that does not consider the costs of deployments for exercises or of maintaining the airlift and sealift capabilities required to deploy U.S.-based forces if and when they are needed overseas (Michael J. Lostumbo, Michael J. McNerney, Eric Peltz, Derek Eaton, David R. Frelinger, Victoria A. Greenfield, John Halliday, Patrick Mills, Bruce R. Nardulli, Stacie L. Pettyjohn, Jerry M. Sollinger, and Stephen M. Worman, *Overseas Basing of U.S. Military Forces: An Assessment of Relative Costs and Strategic Benefits*, Santa Monica, Calif.: RAND Corporation, RR-201-OSD, 2013; Patrick Mills, Adam Grissom, Jennifer Kavanagh, Leila Mahnad, and Stephen M. Worman, *A Cost Analysis of the U.S. Air Force Overseas Posture: Informing Strategic Choices*, Santa Monica, Calif.: RAND Corporation, RR-150-AF, 2013).

[49] Emma Ashford, interview with the authors, video call, August 25, 2021; Eric Gomez, interview with the authors, video call, August 20, 2021; Posen, 2014.

[50] Eugene Gholz, interview with the authors, video call, April 30, 2021; Gholz, Friedman, and Gjoza, 2020.

[51] The interviews took place in April, May, and August 2021. We identified interlocutors with diverse positions within the restraint community according to their published statements regarding U.S. strategy in Asia. We included individuals from each of the ideal-type categories along the range identified in Priebe et al., 2021. We have withheld the names of some interviewees who preferred to remain anonymous.

sions that the United States might want the military to carry out if the United States were to adopt a grand strategy of restraint (Figure 1.2). From there, we identify three scenarios in which the use of force against China would plausibly be consistent with the tenets of restraint and assess the posture required to meet U.S. objectives in those scenarios. Given our focus on regional posture in the Asia-Pacific, we do not detail the space and cyber dimensions of the U.S. military response, since these capabilities are less tied to geography. The remainder of this section describes why we adopted a scenario-based planning approach and how we selected and analyzed the scenarios.

Scenario-Based Planning

DoD regularly uses defense planning scenarios to inform force planning.[52] For example, the United States prioritized preparing for a conflict with the Soviet Union in Europe during the Cold War, but it also identified a series of other scenarios that warranted attention, such as war with China or an intervention in Latin America.[53] Similarly, the 2014 Quadrennial Defense Review outlined a series of scenarios involving Russia, China, North Korea, and Iran to inform U.S. force planning efforts.[54]

FIGURE 1.2
Force Planning Methodology

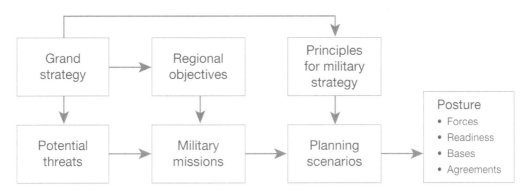

---

[52] Michael Mazarr, Katharina Ley Best, Burgess Laird, Eric V. Larson, Michael E. Linick, and Dan Madden, *The U.S. Department of Defense's Planning Process: Components and Challenges*, Santa Monica, Calif.: RAND Corporation, RR-2173/2-A, 2019; Evan Braden Montgomery, *Defense Planning for the Long Haul: Scenarios, Operational Concepts, and the Future Security Environment*, Washington, D.C.: Center for Strategic and Budgetary Assessments, 2009, pp. 13–18.

[53] Eric V. Larson, *Force Planning Scenarios, 1945–2016: Their Origins and Use in Defense Strategic Planning*, Santa Monica, Calif.: RAND Corporation, RR-2173/1-A, 2019, p. xvi.

[54] Larson, 2019, p. 231.

The chief advantage of using such scenarios in defense planning is that it provides a *rational* basis for developing and maintaining certain military capabilities and not others.[55] U.S. interests are sufficiently expansive that it would be unaffordable to build forces that can counter all conceivable threats to them, so scenario-based planning offers a means to focus on key priorities and determine what capabilities are (and are not) necessary to protect vital interests from the most-salient threats.[56]

Other approaches to defense planning begin with supply rather than demand. These approaches typically take the form of a budgetary limit on defense investment; that amount is then allocated to building and maintaining a set of desired forces or capabilities according to some combination of doctrinal preference, strategic culture and tradition, and political and organizational inertia perpetuating existing force structure.[57] Such a capability- and resource-based defense planning approach can identify what forces the United States can afford to maintain given certain fiscal constraints, and policymakers can then base decisions about security commitments on the capability and capacity limits of the resulting force structure. We focus instead on identifying what restrainers envision as important threats to U.S. interests in Asia and then evaluating what kinds of capabilities and other investments would be needed to deal with them, an approach that is consistent with restrainers' arguments that grand strategy should begin with a rigorous assessment of national interests and that the United States should not build a large military simply because it can afford to do so.[58] This can help determine exactly how limited (or expansive) the means of a grand strategy of restraint would need to be to accomplish its ends.

Scenario-based planning does have potential shortcomings. Planning scenarios rest on specific assumptions about what contingencies are most likely to occur and how each conflict would unfold, and there is a risk that these expectations will be incorrect, especially when planning beyond the immediate future.[59] If the assumptions do turn out to be wrong, forces that have been optimized to fit the demands of particular scenarios at the expense of preparing for other conflicts or for different assumptions about the same scenarios may result in disappointment or defeat. Planning against a large number of possible scenarios and incorporating sensitivity analysis to account for the many potential ways in which a particular conflict might develop is desirable, but this can inflate force planning requirements and distract analytic attention from the most-important priorities.[60] Selecting and develop-

---

[55] Mazarr et al., 2019, p. 6.

[56] Larson, 2019, p. xiii.

[57] Mazarr et al., 2019, pp. 14–16.

[58] Combining threat-based and resource-based approaches is possible. For example, in his force structure proposal, Posen caps defense spending at 2.5 percent of gross domestic product. He then assesses how to allocate those resources given the potential threats that the United States faces (Posen, 2014, p. 135).

[59] Zalmay Khalilzad and David Ochmanek, "Rethinking US Defence Planning," *Survival*, Vol. 39, No. 1, Spring 1997, pp. 46–49; Mazarr et al., 2019, pp. 12–14.

[60] Montgomery, 2009, p. 14.

ing detailed planning scenarios also tends to be a time- and labor-intensive process (as does developing operational plans for them), especially in a defense establishment as large as that of the United States, which leads to trade-offs between scenario quantity and quality. At a minimum, it is important to consider whether one's planning scenarios reflect the full range of contingencies for which the armed forces need to prepare and to acknowledge that the real world may deviate from the scenario designers' script. We detail the assumptions behind our scenarios so that future research can examine how the conclusions might change with different assumptions.

Identifying Candidate Planning Scenarios for a Grand Strategy of Restraint

We focus on potential contingencies involving major conflicts between the United States and China that might plausibly occur in or before the early 2030s, thus requiring preparations within the next decade. We do not suggest that all advocates of restraint would agree that each of these scenarios represents a war that would be worth fighting (or that all advocates of restraint would unconditionally agree to fight a particular war without first considering the particular context when the situation arose). Rather, we identified scenarios that are consistent with at least some visions of restraint and that therefore provide a reasonable starting point for discussing the specific force posture requirements for a grand strategy of restraint in the Asia-Pacific. Our premise is that identifying and examining scenarios in which the logic of restraint *would* recommend going to war is an essential part of translating strategic theory into practical policy proposals. If restrainers reject that any plausible scenarios would justify U.S. military action (and, therefore, peacetime preparation) in the policy-relevant future, then they need to explain why the United States should not completely eliminate its ability to project conventional military power.

Developing Scenarios and Identifying Implications for U.S. Posture

We conducted a preliminary analysis of each of the scenarios to identify broad implications for U.S. posture in the Asia-Pacific under a grand strategy of restraint. In particular, for each scenario, we sought to

- describe potential Chinese military strategies
- describe potential U.S. and allied military strategies
- identify capabilities that the United States and its allies would need to meet U.S. objectives
- identify key elements of regional posture that would support the U.S. and allied strategy.

To do this, we combined literature reviews and expert roundtables to generate a first cut at each of these issues. For each scenario, we conducted a literature review of relevant U.S., Japanese, and Chinese military capabilities and operational approaches. We then held a structured discussion with a group of RAND researchers with expertise in U.S., U.S. ally and partner, and Chinese capabilities and approaches to warfighting. The group included experts with specialized backgrounds on each of the U.S. services and joint military operations.[61] These roundtables took place during June and July 2021. The roundtable discussions focused on how China might approach the scenario, how the United States and its allies would approach it, and what the implications for U.S. capabilities and posture would be. The research team used these expert perspectives to inform a more detailed review of the literature and analysis of how each scenario might unfold.

Future research on these scenarios (or other scenarios put forward by restrainers) should involve modeling or wargaming to develop more-detailed implications for U.S. posture. This preliminary analysis focuses on current military technology and systems that analysts expect the United States, China, and Japan to deploy in the near term. Future analysis should consider the potential implications of emerging technologies, including advances in space, cyber, electronic warfare, and artificial intelligence that could change China's capacity to dominate the region, how the United States and Japan could counter regional threats, or the underlying risks and dynamics of escalation in a potential conflict.[62]

---

[61] The same core group of experts participated in each of the three roundtables. We added an expert on island defenses for the Ryukyu Islands scenario. An expert in the Japanese military attended the roundtables on two of the scenarios: the one focusing on the defense of the Ryukyus and one involving a major Chinese attack on the Japanese homeland and military.

[62] For discussions of Chinese concepts for integrating artificial intelligence, see Edmund J. Burke, Kristen Gunness, Cortez A. Cooper III, and Mark Cozad, *People's Liberation Army Operational Concepts*, Santa Monica, Calif.: RAND Corporation, RR-A394-1, 2020, p. 22; and Yuan Yi [袁艺], "Will AI Command Future Wars?" ["人工智能将指挥未来战争?"], *Defense Daily* [中国国防报], January 12, 2017.

CHAPTER TWO

Operationalizing Restraint in the Asia-Pacific

In this report, we seek to translate the theoretical principles of restraint into concrete policy implications for U.S. strategy in the Asia-Pacific. Because restraint is a grand strategy, restrainers offer recommendations at a relatively high level of generality. But understanding the trade-offs among alternative U.S. strategies requires a sense of how policymakers would actually implement restraint in practice, which could vary widely depending on the region in question.[1] For example, advocates of restraint often argue that the United States should withdraw its military presence from Europe because European states are wealthy enough that they could join together to balance against threats from Russia.[2] By contrast, many restrainers believe that the United States cannot fully retrench from Asia. China is more powerful than Russia, and the security ties among U.S. allies and partners in the region are weaker, so many realist advocates of restraint call for the United States to help allies and partners in Asia maintain a regional balance of power against China.[3]

Drawing on restrainers' writings and extrapolating from the theoretical principles that inform the logic of restraint, in this chapter, we identify restrainers' objectives in the Asia-Pacific region, potential threats to those objectives, and the associated military missions that the United States may want to be able to conduct under a grand strategy of restraint. We conclude the chapter by proposing candidate scenarios that could inform DoD planning under this type of strategy.

This chapter, like the larger report, is intended to begin a conversation about these more detailed aspects of restraint. As restrainers continue to develop their strategies and engage with this proposed framework, their views may evolve or may become more concrete than

---

[1] For an overview of how the United States might implement a strategy of restraint, see Priebe et al., 2021. This report further develops the details on the varieties of restraint and the potential implications for U.S. force posture in Asia because it is the region that restrainers acknowledge poses the most difficult case for retrenchment.

[2] Barry Posen, "Europe Can Defend Itself," *Survival*, Vol. 62, No. 6, December 2020–January 2021.

[3] Mearsheimer and Walt, 2016; Posen, 2014, p. 91. Some realists call for complete withdrawal and do not believe that maintaining a regional balance of power is always necessary to protect vital U.S. interests. See, for example, Layne, 2006, pp. 186–190. More recently, Layne has called for accommodating China's interests as the country rises (Christopher Layne, "Coming Storms: The Return of Great-Power War," *Foreign Affairs*, Vol. 99, No. 6, November–December 2020). His argument seems to follow the same logic as his past work.

in the past. Therefore, the discussions here are not the final word about the military implications of restraint for the region, but they reflect our best understanding of the strategy as it is currently formulated.

U.S. Objectives for the Asia-Pacific Region

As discussed in Chapter One, restrainers want to reserve the use of military force for protecting only a limited number of vital interests.[4] Although restrainers care about a variety of other interests, they prefer to pursue them using nonmilitary instruments of national power, which they view as less costly and generally more effective.[5] Given this overarching perspective, the following are the most important objectives for the Asia-Pacific region that restrainers explicitly identify as priorities or that implicitly flow from their strategic logic (Table 2.1).

Protect the U.S. homeland and territories from attack by potential adversaries in Asia. Restrainers uniformly agree that preventing other countries from occupying or attacking any part of the U.S. homeland is a vital interest.[6] Although restrainers do not explicitly say as much, we assume that they would also seek to protect U.S. territories in the Pacific, including Guam, the Northern Mariana Islands, and American Samoa.

Preserve the U.S. ability to operate and trade in Pacific areas outside the first island chain. Advocates of restraint prefer that the United States retain the ability to move military forces globally and trade with the rest of the world, including with China, to support U.S. prosperity.[7] Restrainers therefore want to be able to prevent other countries from imposing a blockade on U.S. maritime commerce with major trading partners in the Pacific or interdicting trade in the sea lanes that connect the Pacific Ocean to the Indian Ocean. This means that no country should be able to deny the United States military or commercial access to the Pacific Ocean, the Philippine Sea, the Sea of Japan, or any other area outside what China refers to as the *first island chain*—which Chinese writings define as bounding the East China

---

[4] Gholz, Press, and Sapolsky, 1997; Posen, 2014; Stephen M. Walt, *Taming American Power: The Global Response to U.S. Primacy*, New York: W. W. Norton & Company, 2006.

[5] Alexander B. Downes and Jonathan Monten, "Does Spreading Democracy by Force Have a Place in US Grand Strategy? A Skeptical View," in A. Trevor Thrall and Benjamin H. Friedman, eds., *US Grand Strategy in the 21st Century: The Case for Restraint*, New York: Routledge, 2018; Gholz, Press, and Sapolsky, 1997, p. 10; Walt, 2018a, pp. 271–272.

[6] Advocate of restraint A, interview with the authors, video call, May 6, 2021; Emma Ashford, interview with the authors, video call, August 25, 2021; Jasen J. Castillo, interview with the authors, video call, May 3, 2021; Eric Gomez, interview with the authors, video call, August 20, 2021. See, for example, John Glaser, Christopher A. Preble, and A. Trevor Thrall, "Towards a More Prudent American Grand Strategy," *Survival*, Vol. 61, No. 5, 2019, p. 30; and Posen, 2014, p. 10.

[7] Emma Ashford, interview with the authors, video call, August 25, 2021; Gholz, Press, and Sapolsky, 1997, pp. 5–6, 30; Colin Grabow, *Responsible Stakeholders: Why the United States Should Welcome China's Economic Leadership*, Washington, D.C.: Cato Institute, Policy Analysis No. 821, October 3, 2017; Posen, 2003; Posen, 2014; Walt, 2018b, p. 13.

TABLE 2.1

Key U.S. Military Objectives in the Asia-Pacific Under Alternative Visions of Restraint

Objective	Defensive Restraint	Flexible Restraint	Counter-hegemonic Restraint	Current U.S. Grand Strategy
Protect the U.S. homeland and territories from attack by potential adversaries in Asia				
Preserve the U.S. ability to operate and trade in Pacific areas outside the first island chain				
Maintain Japan's independence as a major power				
Maintain South Korea's independence				
Maintain the independence of other treaty allies				
Prevent the forcible Chinese conquest of Taiwan			See note a	
Preserve U.S. freedom to operate and trade in the East China, South China, and Yellow seas				
Defend allies' claims to disputed maritime areas in the South and East China seas				
Prevent nuclear proliferation				
Demonstrate U.S. reliability as a security provider to allies and partners				

NOTES: Dark blue cells indicate vital U.S. security interests that are worth fighting for if success appears achievable. Lighter blue cells indicate security interests that are worth defending by force if costs are reasonable. Beige cells indicate objectives that force would not be used to achieve. Restrainers often call for a multiyear transition from current U.S. commitments to these preferred outcomes. The list of objectives for post–Cold War U.S. grand strategy is not comprehensive. The "current U.S. grand strategy" column also represents the views of restrainers who advocate restraint in other regions but not in the Asia-Pacific.
a Some restrainers would favor defending Taiwan if the costs of doing so were low but argue that it is unrealistic to imagine that they would be.

Sea, South China Sea, and Yellow Sea (Figure 2.1)—or to deny U.S. access to the airspace above these waters.[8]

Restrainers differ, however, over the importance of this objective. For defensive restrainers, protecting U.S. maritime trade is an important objective but not necessarily one that is worth fighting a major war to protect. In their view, the United States' large and diverse economy and its many trading partners in the Western Hemisphere and across the Atlantic would insulate it from economic ruin even if its trade with East Asia ceased. Defensive restrainers

---

[8]   While China's conceptualization of what is included in the first island chain varies by source, Chinese writings all include the East China Sea, South China Sea, and Yellow Sea in their definitions (Andrew S. Erickson and Joel Wuthnow, "Barriers, Springboards and Benchmarks: China Conceptualizes the Pacific 'Island Chains,'" *China Quarterly*, Vol. 225, March 2016). China's official strategy statements refer to these three seas as China's "offshore waters." See, for example, "Document: China's Military Strategy," USNI News, last updated May 26, 2015.

FIGURE 2.1

The First and Second Island Chains

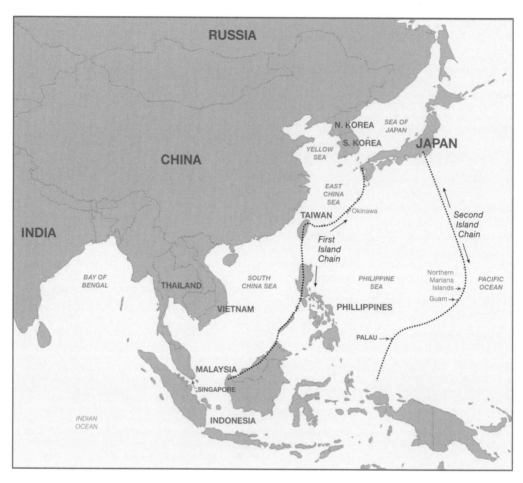

note that trade with countries in the Asia-Pacific makes up a relatively small share of U.S. gross domestic product (Table 2.2).[9] Moreover, they argue, even if an adversary could maintain such a disruption to U.S. trade with Asia over the long term—suffering its own economic costs in the process—the effects on the U.S. economy would wane over time because the United States would innovate and adapt its supply chains.[10] In contrast, counterhegemonic restrainers would be less sanguine about tolerating disruptions to trade in the Pacific because

---

[9] Eugene Gholz, interview with the authors, video call, April 30, 2021. Posen shares this view (see Posen, 2014, p. 63).

[10] Eugene Gholz, interview with the authors, video call, April 30, 2021; Eugene Gholz and Daryl G. Press, "The Effects of Wars on Neutral Countries: Why It Doesn't Pay to Preserve the Peace," *Security Studies*, Vol. 10, No. 4, Summer 2001.

TABLE 2.2

U.S. Trade in Goods with Key Maritime States in East and Southeast Asia, 2020

Country	Percentage of Total U.S. Trade	Percentage of Total U.S. Gross Domestic Product
China	17.2	2.7
Japan	5.6	0.9
South Korea	3.9	0.6
Vietnam	2.8	0.4
Taiwan	2.8	0.4
Singapore	1.8	0.3
Malaysia	1.7	0.3
Thailand	1.5	0.2
Indonesia	0.9	0.1
Philippines	0.6	0.1
Cambodia	0.2	0.0
Total (excluding China)	**21.8**	**3.3**
Total (including China)	**39.0**	**6.0**

SOURCES: Values are calculated from data in Bureau of Economic Analysis, "Gross Domestic Product, (Third Estimate), GDP by Industry, and Corporate Profits, Fourth Quarter and Year 2020," news release, U.S. Department of Commerce, March 25, 2021; and U.S. Census Bureau, "U.S. Trade in Goods by Country," webpage, undated.

the economic effects could harm the U.S. power position and seriously weaken regional states that are opposed to China.

Maintain Japan's independence as a major power. Advocates of restraint care about the future of Japan and prefer that it remain an independent power that is capable of resisting coercive pressure from Beijing for several reasons.[11] First, because Japan is a wealthy industrial power, China's being able to direct Japan's economy and foreign policy to serve its own ends would significantly enhance China's power (although restrainers are not of one mind about whether China could actually bend Japan to its will).[12] Second, Japan's geography and military capabilities make it an obstacle to China's ability to dominate the air and maritime space within the first island chain and hinder the ability of the People's Liberation Army (PLA) to project power with impunity into the Pacific so long as Japan remains indepen-

---

[11] Emma Ashford, interview with the authors, video call, August 25, 2021; Eric Gomez, interview with the authors, video call, August 20, 2021.

[12] Posen, 2014, p. 98. On the feasibility of subjugating economies built on information technology, see Stephen G. Brooks, "The Globalization of Production and the Changing Benefits of Conquest," *Journal of Conflict Resolution*, Vol. 43, No. 5, October 1999. See also Peter Liberman, *Does Conquest Pay? The Exploitation of Occupied Industrial Societies*, Princeton, N.J.: Princeton University Press, 1996.

dent and not aligned with Beijing.[13] Third, having another major power nearby keeps China's attention in its own neighborhood, making it less able to interfere in the Americas or in other regions in which the United States has interests.[14]

Advocates of restraint therefore prefer that Japan not suffer a decisive military loss at the hands of China or otherwise lose control of strategic parts of its territory or its foreign policy autonomy. Restrainers are unwilling to be the primary provider of Japan's security, but flexible and counterhegemonic restrainers would be willing to fight to assist Japan in a war that threatened its independence.[15]

Defensive restrainers, however, are skeptical that the loss of Japanese independence would jeopardize U.S. security, since it would not alter the fundamental defensive advantages that the United States enjoys. Moreover, they doubt that China could subjugate a hostile Japan and direct its resources in ways that would significantly enhance Chinese power. Defensive restrainers are therefore unwilling to use force to defend Japan. They prefer instead to help Japan increase its self-defense capabilities through weapon sales or subsidies.[16]

Maintain South Korea's independence. Maintaining the independence of South Korea is another objective over which restrainers disagree because of different views on both the importance of South Korea to U.S. security and the threat that it faces. Counterhegemonic restrainers consider South Korea to be a sufficiently important national interest to fight for if necessary because of its wealth and industrial capability, which make it a significant strategic counterweight against China.[17] Therefore, counterhegemonic restrainers agree with current U.S. policymakers that the United States should defend South Korea against an attack by North Korea.[18] Flexible restrainers support maintaining an alliance with South Korea to counter China but argue that South Korea is wealthy enough to develop and maintain the military capabilities it needs to defend itself from a North Korean invasion on its own. These restrainers call for a gradual U.S. withdrawal to give South Korea time to develop the capabilities, possibly including nuclear capabilities, that it needs. We interpret this as meaning that flexible restrainers see South Korean independence as an objective in theory but do not

---

[13] Posen, 2014, p. 99.

[14] Jasen J. Castillo, interview with the authors, video call, May 3, 2021; John J. Mearsheimer, *The Tragedy of Great Power Politics*, New York: W. W. Norton & Company, 2001, p. 365; Walt, 2018a, p. 262; Walt, 2018b, p. 13.

[15] Jasen J. Castillo, interview with the authors, video call, May 3, 2021; Posen, 2014.

[16] Eugene Gholz, interview with the authors, video call, April 30, 2021.

[17] Emma Ashford, interview with the authors, video call, August 25, 2021; Castillo, 2019, p. 31; Eric Gomez, interview with the authors, video call, August 20, 2021.

[18] For the general principle that the United States must deter and defeat aggression against allies in both the Biden and Trump administrations, see National Security Council, 2018; and White House, 2021, p. 9. Context on the Trump-era strategic framework document is provided in Robert C. O'Brien, "A Free and Open Indo-Pacific," White House, January 5, 2021. An advocate of retrenchment from Europe and the Middle East to shift resources to Asia also supports this as a U.S. objective (Advocate of restraint B, interview with the authors, video call, May 14, 2021).

perceive a serious threat to it today.[19] Defensive restrainers tend to agree that South Korea can handle any threats posed by North Korea and further argue for ending U.S. alliances, including with South Korea, believing that they incentivize allies to underinvest in their own defense and are not central to U.S. security.[20]

Restrainers agree that some objectives are not worth fighting for. One of the distinguishing features that separates restraint from recent U.S. grand strategy is the narrow scope that it applies to defining vital interests. Restrainers agree with some aspects of recent U.S. grand strategy, including defending the U.S. homeland, ensuring access to global markets, and retaining a favorable balance of power in Asia.[21] Some restrainers also support the continued presence of U.S. forces for the defense of South Korea and Japan.[22] Despite these overlapping conceptions of regional objectives, restrainers may care about some of the same objectives for different reasons. For example, current U.S. policymakers typically value defending Japan in part because the United States has made a commitment to do so, whereas restrainers care about it solely because of its implications for the balance of power.[23] In other cases, restrainers are not willing to pay as high a cost as recent U.S. policymakers would have, or to rely on military power to the same extent, to defend national interests that they consider less than truly vital.

Taiwan's independence is an area of conspicuous difference between restrainers and U.S. policymakers. The United States has a policy of strategic ambiguity regarding Taiwan, under which it has no formal commitment to come to Taiwan's defense but is required under the Taiwan Relations Act to maintain the capability to do so. The same law states that any attempt to conquer Taiwan would be of "grave concern" to the United States.[24] Although strategic ambiguity remains official U.S. policy, policymakers have often stated or implied that the United States would come to Taiwan's defense if it were attacked.[25] Moreover, U.S. official statements point to the U.S. interest in maintaining the regional order, upholding the

---

[19] Posen, 2014, pp. 104–105.

[20] Doug Bandow, "It's Time for America to Cut South Korea Loose," *Foreign Policy*, April 13, 2017; Benjamin H. Friedman, *Bad Idea: Permanent Alliances*, Defense 360, Washington, D.C.: Center for Strategic and International Studies, December 2018; Benjamin H. Friedman and Justin Logan, "Why the U.S. Military Budget Is 'Foolish and Sustainable,'" *Orbis*, Vol. 56, No. 2, Spring 2012, pp. 180–181.

[21] The Biden administration seems to share these objectives with restrainers, as well as an emphasis on reducing U.S. overreliance on the use of force. See, especially, White House, 2021, pp. 9, 14. The Trump administration shared these objectives related to defending the homeland, maintaining a favorable balance of power, and ensuring access to the global commons (DoD, 2019, pp. 3–4, 15–16; Mattis, 2018, p. 4; National Security Council, 2018, p. 1; U.S. Department of State, 2019, pp. 22–23; White House, 2017, pp. 4, 45–47).

[22] DoD, 2019, pp. 23, 25; White House, 2017, p. 47.

[23] Posen, 2014.

[24] Public Law 96-8, Taiwan Relations Act, January 1, 1979.

[25] See, for example, David E. Sanger, "Biden Said the U.S. Would Protect Taiwan. But It's Not That Clear-Cut," *New York Times*, October 22, 2021. For other statements about the Biden administration's support for Taiwan, see Alex Leary and Bob Davis, "Biden's China Policy Is Emerging—And It Looks a Lot Like

norms of sovereignty and territorial integrity, and defending democracy, all of which would be under threat should China forcibly reunify with Taiwan.[26] Such concerns do not generally motivate advocates of restraint. Some restrainers do support maintaining strategic ambiguity regarding U.S. willingness to fight for Taiwan, at least in the short term.[27] But, in the longer term, they are generally unwilling to fight a war with China over Taiwan.[28]

Restrainers acknowledge that there are similar types of strategic advantages to Taiwan's *de facto* independence as with Japan's, albeit on a smaller scale, and see Taiwan as a laudable democracy.[29] So, they generally support helping Taiwan become as hard as possible for China to attack, such as by selling or giving Taiwan weapons to increase its ability to defend itself.[30] However, they are unwilling to fight to defend the island directly because they worry about the costs and potential escalatory risks of the United States fighting China in a location so close to China's shores and over an interest that Beijing considers so vital. For example, they worry that the United States would engage in strikes on mainland China in a conflict over Taiwan, which could increase the risk of nuclear escalation. Restrainers also believe that China cares more deeply about Taiwan than about other issues, such as disputes in the South and East China seas. As a result, restrainers expect that it will be harder to deter China from trying to conquer Taiwan and that China would be more willing to accept significant costs and risks to retake Taiwan than it would over other issues. Restrainers also note that China's views on Taiwan are well known, whereas it is unclear whether China would attack Japan's main islands or the Ryukyus. Although the loss of Taiwan might have implications for Japan's security if China becomes more ambitious in the future, restrainers are unwilling to accept the costs and risks of defending Taiwan for this theoretical threat to an interest (Japan) that restrainers care more about.[31]

Restrainers also take a different view from current U.S. defense policy over whether the United States should use military force to maintain freedom of movement and operations inside the first island chain, including the ability to freely transit the Taiwan Strait, the South China Sea, and the East China Sea (Figure 2.1).[32] All things being equal, restrainers prefer to

---

Trump's," *Wall Street Journal*, June 10, 2021; White House, 2021, p. 21. For the Trump administration's policy, see National Security Council, 2018, p. 7.

[26] Michael Mazza, "Why Defending Taiwan Is an American Political Consensus," American Enterprise Institute, Global Taiwan Institute, November 4, 2020.

[27] Eric Gomez, interview with the authors, video call, August 20, 2021.

[28] Emma Ashford, interview with the authors, video call, August 25, 2021; Posen, 2014.

[29] Advocate of restraint A, interview with the authors, video call, May 6, 2021.

[30] Ted Galen Carpenter and Eric Gomez, "East Asia and a Strategy of Restraint," *War on the Rocks*, August 10, 2016; Gholz, Friedman, and Gjoza, 2020; Porter, 2018, p. 127.

[31] Emma Ashford, interview with the authors, video call, August 25, 2021; Eric Gomez, interview with the authors, video call, August 20, 2021; Posen, 2014, p. 104.

[32] DoD defines *freedom of the seas* as "all the rights, freedoms, and lawful uses of the sea and airspace, including for military ships and aircraft, recognized under international law" (U.S. Navy, U.S. Marine

be able to trade freely globally. However, they are not willing to fight to ensure U.S. access in all areas. In particular, many advocates of restraint are willing to accept China's ability to deny the United States military and commercial access to these areas near China's coast.[33] They acknowledge that China could disrupt trade with some countries if China controlled this area but argue that many commercial vessels and U.S. military forces could use alternative routes should China attempt to limit access to major sea lines of communication (SLOCs) through the South China Sea.[34] Given these alternatives, restrainers do not believe that the United States should bear a high cost or court significant risk to guarantee access to maritime areas of limited interest to the United States that are so close and vital to its principal major power rival.[35]

Relatedly, restrainers and recent U.S. administrations differ over whether the United States should use force to defend allies' claims in disputed areas within the first island chain. The Trump administration assured the Philippines and Japan that U.S. treaty commitments would apply in the case of Chinese attacks on allied forces or defense of their maritime claims in the South and East China seas.[36] The Biden administration has reaffirmed these commitments.[37] Restrainers, by contrast, are generally not willing to fight to protect the maritime

---

Corps, and U.S. Coast Guard, *Advantage at Sea: Prevailing with Integrated All-Domain Naval Power*, Washington, D.C., December 2020, p. 25). The Navy's recently published maritime strategy states that freedom of the seas is one of the objectives for U.S. naval presence in the Asia-Pacific region (U.S. Navy, U.S. Marine Corps, and U.S. Coast Guard, 2020, pp. 13–14). For the Trump administration's policy in this area, see National Security Council, 2018, p. 7. In a difference from his general agreement with the Biden administration's objectives in the region, an advocate of restraint in Europe and the Middle East to shift resources to the Asia-Pacific argued that the United States needed only to prevent China from obtaining command in this area, not sustain U.S. access (Advocate of restraint B, interview with the authors, video call, May 14, 2021).

[33] Advocate of restraint A, interview with the authors, video call, May 6, 2021; Jasen J. Castillo, interview with the authors, video call, May 3, 2021. This view is also implied by the logic of defensive restraint (Eugene Gholz, interview with the authors, video call, April 30, 2021). Ashford disagrees, arguing that the United States should retain the ability to fight in this area if needed to ensure that South Korea can receive trade, especially energy imports (Emma Ashford, interview with the authors, video call, August 25, 2021).

[34] Eugene Gholz, interview with the authors, video call, April 30, 2021.

[35] Posen refers to such maritime areas as the *contested zone* (Posen, 2003; Posen, 2014).

[36] DoD, 2019, pp. 29, 43; Steve Holland and Kiyoshi Takenaka, "Trump Says U.S. Committed to Japan Security, in Change from Campaign Rhetoric," Reuters, February 10, 2017; National Security Council, 2018, p. 7.

[37] In the East China Sea, the United States has specifically named the Senkaku Islands as falling within the scope of its defense commitments to Japan. The scope of the original treaty with the Philippines includes responding to an "armed attack on the metropolitan territory of either of the Parties, or on the island territories under its jurisdiction in the Pacific or on its armed forces, public vessels or aircraft in the Pacific" (Mark Nevitt, "The US-Philippines Defense Treaty and the Pompeo Doctrine on South China Sea," *Just Security*, March 11, 2019). The United States has clarified that the "Pacific area" specified in its treaty with the Philippines includes the South China Sea, but it has not named specific territorial features that it is committed to defending ("Biden Backs Trump Rejection of China's South China Sea Claim," *Politico*, July 11, 2021; Nevitt, 2019; "U.S.-Japan Joint Leaders' Statement: 'U.S.–Japan Global Partnership for a New Era,'" press release, White House, April 16, 2021).

claims of U.S. allies and partners in the South or East China seas, including Japan's control of the Senkaku/Diaoyu Islands. They assess that these islands are strategically inconsequential.[38]

Advocates of restraint have not written much about whether the United States should be willing to use force to defend the homelands of other countries in the region beyond Japan and South Korea.[39] Current U.S. policy is to defend allies and partners in the region.[40] The underlying logic of restraint suggests that restrainers would likely take a different view. Defensive restrainers seek to end U.S. alliances in the region, so they would presumably oppose defending any country in the Asia-Pacific. Flexible and counterhegemonic restrainers might prefer that the Philippines and Indonesia remain outside China's control because their independence makes it harder for China to project maritime power into the open ocean. If China were to occupy these countries or coerce them into aligning with it, the PLA could use these territories to project naval power. However, advocates of restraint expect that nationalism in these countries, as well as their size and location, would make it unlikely that China that could achieve this objective in the foreseeable future.[41] If China were to seek to gain military access to territory belonging to these countries through coercion rather than conquest, a flexible restrainer whom we interviewed argued that United States should rely only on nonmilitary tools to resist it.[42]

Restrainers share a deep-seated skepticism about the use of military interventions to demonstrate the willingness of the United States to uphold its commitments.[43] They argue that potential adversaries make calculations about the credibility of the United States that are based on its interests in a particular context and its capabilities to protect those interests rather than its past actions elsewhere.[44] U.S. inaction in one context, according to this logic, does not necessarily lead states to doubt U.S. credibility in other cases. For example, advocates of restraint reject the claim that ending the war in Afghanistan undermined U.S. cred-

---

[38] Emma Ashford, interview with the authors, video call, August 25, 2021; Jasen J. Castillo, interview with the authors, video call, May 3, 2021. On the Senkaku/Diaoyu Islands, see Ted Galen Carpenter, "Washington Needs to Jettison Its Commitment to Defend the Senkakus," Cato Institute, January 9, 2020. For a technical analysis of the military implications of China's position in the South China Sea, see Shahryar Pasandideh, "Do China's New Islands Allow It to Militarily Dominate the South China Sea?" *Asian Security*, Vol. 17, No. 1, 2021.

[39] Priebe et al., 2021.

[40] White House, 2021, p. 9. An advocate of retrenchment from Europe and the Middle East to shift resources to Asia also noted that he would support the defense of the Philippines against a Chinese attack (Advocate of restraint B, interview with the authors, video call, May 14, 2021).

[41] Posen, 2014, pp. 95, 99.

[42] Advocate of restraint A, interview with the authors, video call, May 6, 2021.

[43] Layne, 2006, p. 160; Walt, 2015.

[44] For evidence in support of this claim, restrainers often point to Press, 2005.

ibility in East Asia because the contexts of counterterrorism campaigns in the Middle East and great-power competition in the Asia-Pacific are so different.[45]

Restrainers also argue that preventive war is rarely an appropriate remedy to concerns about nuclear proliferation and instead call for relying on multilateral pressure and deterrence to protect the United States from states that do acquire nuclear capabilities.[46] Advocates of restraint acknowledge that withdrawing U.S. forces could encourage South Korea and Japan to develop a nuclear deterrent, but they believe that such programs would help those countries better provide for their own defense.[47] In contrast, U.S. policymakers have often stated that nonproliferation is a vital U.S. interest and at various times have seriously considered using force to prevent the spread of nuclear weapons.[48]

Threats from China

In this section, we assess threats to the regional objectives outlined above during the next ten years. We focus particularly on the threat that China poses. Russia has power-projection capabilities that enable it to conduct long-range strikes in the Indo-Pacific region.[49] This includes the ability to strike the U.S. homeland with intercontinental ballistic missiles (ICBMs) and submarine-launched ballistic missiles (SLBMs), cruise missiles, long-range bombers, and cyberattacks against critical infrastructure.[50] However, most of Russia's military capabilities are focused on defending the Russian homeland and maintaining influence over the countries of the former Soviet Union rather than dominating the Eurasian region more broadly.[51] We do not address North Korea, since its power-projection capabilities are more limited and

---

[45] Walt, 2021.

[46] Posen, 2014, pp. 78, 133.

[47] Gholz, Press, and Sapolsky, 1997, pp. 22–23; Posen, 2014, pp. 72–80, 105.

[48] Francis J. Gavin, "Strategies of Inhibition: U.S. Grand Strategy, the Nuclear Revolution, and Nonproliferation," *International Security*, Vol. 40, No. 1, Summer 2015; Nicholas L. Miller, *Stopping the Bomb: The Sources and Effectiveness of US Nonproliferation Policy*, Ithaca, N.Y.: Cornell University Press, 2018; Karl P. Mueller, Jasen J. Castillo, Forrest E. Morgan, Negeen Pegahi, and Brian Rosen, *Striking First: Preemptive and Preventive Attack in U.S. National Security Policy*, Santa Monica, Calif.: RAND Corporation, MG-403-AF, 2006.

[49] William Heerdt, "Russian Hard Power Projection: A Brief Synopsis," blog post, *Post-Soviet Post*, March 25, 2020.

[50] John Grady, "Russia Is Top Military Threat to U.S. Homeland, Air Force General Says," USNI News, August 18, 2021; Office of the Director of National Intelligence, *Annual Threat Assessment of the US Intelligence Community*, Washington, D.C., April 9, 2021, p. 11; Amy F. Woolf, *Russia's Nuclear Weapons: Doctrine, Forces, and Modernization*, Washington, D.C.: Congressional Research Service, R45861, July 2020, p. 13.

[51] Andrew Radin, Lynn E. Davis, Edward Geist, Eugeniu Han, Dara Massicot, Matthew Povlock, Clint Reach, Scott Boston, Samuel Charap, William Mackenzie, Katya Migacheva, Trevor Johnston, and Austin Long, *What Will Russian Military Capabilities Look Like in the Future?* Santa Monica, Calif.: RAND Corporation, RB-10038-A, 2019, pp. 1–2.

since many advocates of restraint believe that the country that North Korea most directly threatens, South Korea, can and should provide for its own defense without U.S. assistance.[52] China's growing military power means that it is the predominant driver of U.S. posture in the region, and it would presumably continue to be so if the United States were to adopt a more restrained grand strategy.

We discuss current Chinese capabilities and those under development that are relevant to China's ability to threaten the U.S. homeland, Japan, South Korea, or the U.S. ability to operate in areas of the Pacific outside the first island chain. We focus primarily on China's capabilities rather than its intentions to understand the full variety of possible threats to U.S. interests given the difficulty of knowing another state's intentions and their potential to change over time. We also consider Japan's capabilities to defend its territory from PLA attacks, as well as some points of comparison between Chinese and Japanese armed forces. The defense planning scenarios in the subsequent chapters provide more-detailed analysis of the potential interactions of forces and how each side might fare in a conflict.

As a general matter, advocates of restraint see China as a long-term threat to the objectives discussed above rather than a significant current threat.[53] Overall, we find that although China's military capabilities are growing, they pose only a limited threat to the U.S. homeland, including Hawaii and Alaska, and we agree with advocates of restraint that China is far from developing a first-strike capability that would undermine the U.S. nuclear deterrent.[54] China's new nuclear-powered submarine capabilities and intermediate-range ballistic missiles (IRBMs) pose more of a threat to the U.S. territories of Guam and the Northern Marianas, as does the Chinese air force's expanding fleet of H-6 bombers, which are armed with air-launched cruise missiles suitable for long-range strikes.[55] Although China will not have the capability in the near term to exert control over a widespread maritime area, its increasing naval and air capabilities will be able to hold U.S. forces at high risk within the first island chain and, to a lesser degree, out to the second island chain.[56] The Chinese military threat to Japan is potentially the most salient for advocates of restraint given Japan's significance as a regional power and its location, which enables China to target nearby Japanese territory

---

[52] The U.S. Intelligence Community assesses that the North Korean missile program poses a threat and that North Korea could "cause temporary, limited disruptions" of critical infrastructure in the United States (Office of the Director of National Intelligence, 2021, p. 15).

[53] Jasen J. Castillo, interview with the authors, video call, May 3, 2021; Eugene Gholz, interview with the authors, video call, April 30, 2021.

[54] China's development of nuclear weapons has generally focused on a second-strike nuclear retaliatory capability rather than a first-strike posture (Tong Zhao, *Modernizing Without Destabilizing: China's Nuclear Posture in a New Era*, Beijing: Carnegie-Tsinghua Center for Global Policy, 2020).

[55] Office of the Secretary of Defense, *Annual Report to Congress: Military and Security Developments Involving the People's Republic of China*, Washington, D.C.: Department of Defense, 2020, p. 51; Office of the Secretary of Defense, *Annual Report to Congress: Military and Security Developments Involving the People's Republic of China 2021*, Washington, D.C.: Department of Defense, 2021, p. 56.

[56] Office of the Secretary of Defense, 2021, p. 77.

relatively easily with such capabilities as the PLA's medium- to long-range missiles, air forces, and naval forces.[57]

Threats to the Physical Security of the United States and Its Territories

Advocates of restraint argue in broad terms that there are few existential threats to the U.S. homeland and territories. The long distances between the United States and other powers, China's limited air and maritime power-projection capabilities, and the caution that nuclear deterrence induces mean that a large-scale physical attack by air, land, maritime, or nuclear forces is very unlikely. Nor do advocates of restraint believe that this type of threat will arise in the near term. Responding to the potential growth of such threats would remain a long-term U.S. interest.[58] This does not mean that restrainers believe that the United States is immune to all attacks, even in the near term. Restrainers accept that major powers will remain capable of harming the United States through such means as nuclear-armed ICBMs but are comfortable relying on deterrence to protect against these attacks. They also argue that U.S. military disengagement and resolving disputes politically would make conflicts that might lead to such attacks less likely.[59]

Advocates of restraint have not written much about space or cyber capabilities.[60] This does not necessarily mean that restrainers see no cause for concern in these areas, but most of their claims about the geographical security of the United States and calls for reducing U.S. overseas presence focus on threats in other domains. Threats in the land, air, and maritime domains rather than from space and cyberspace are the primary drivers behind U.S. decisions about where to base forces and which countries to defend.

Restrainers would be concerned if, in the future, China were to gain a much greater capability to project power across the Pacific Ocean. We assess that China's ability to project maritime power toward the coast of the United States will remain extremely limited within the next decade. Although China is developing some expeditionary maritime capabilities that

---

[57] Office of the Secretary of Defense, 2021, pp. 77–78.

[58] Gholz, Press, and Sapolsky, 1997, p. 8; Layne, 2006, p. 186; Mearsheimer and Walt, 2016; Porter, 2018; Posen, 2014, pp. 19, 135–139.

[59] Posen, 2014, pp. 71–72.

[60] For exceptions, see Joshua Rovner, "Why Restraint in the Real World Encourages Digital Espionage," *War on the Rocks*, December 8, 2021; and Brandon Valeriano and Benjamin Jensen, *The Myth of the Cyber Offense: The Case for Restraint*, Washington, D.C.: CATO Institute, Policy Analysis No. 862, January 15, 2019. For analysis from researchers who are not restrainers but come to similar conclusions as some restrainers about the limits of cyberwarfare's offensive potential, see Erik Gartzke, "The Myth of Cyberwar: Bringing War in Cyberspace Back Down to Earth," *International Security*, Vol. 38, No. 2, Fall 2013; and Rebecca Slayton, "What Is the Cyber Offense-Defense Balance? Conceptions, Causes, and Assessment," *International Security*, Vol. 41, No. 3, Winter 2016–2017.

can, in theory, allow the military to project power across the Pacific Ocean, including aircraft carriers and nuclear-powered submarines, these are still nascent.[61]

Restrainers would also be concerned if China were to develop the ability to threaten the survivability of the nuclear forces that give the United States an assured retaliatory capability. This might include the development of highly effective missile defenses that could destroy incoming U.S. nuclear missiles or a massive increase in the number of Chinese nuclear warheads and launch capabilities, along with improved intelligence, surveillance, and reconnaissance (ISR) and anti-submarine warfare (ASW) that would allow China to conduct a disabling first strike against the United States.

Restrainers, and defense analysts generally, assess that there is no near-term prospect of either development.[62] China is far from developing a first-strike capability that could undermine U.S. nuclear deterrence. Although it is expanding, China's nuclear arsenal remains relatively small compared with the U.S. arsenal, so China could not conduct a disarming first strike, even against U.S. land-based nuclear forces alone.[63] China is also investing in improved ASW capabilities, but these remain far from posing a significant threat to U.S. ballistic missile submarines operating far from Chinese shores.[64] Furthermore, although the PLA is in the process of developing ballistic missile defense capabilities to intercept IRBMs and eventually ICBMs, it does not have a robust national missile defense system to protect itself against such weapons (nor does any other country), and this is unlikely to change in the near future.[65] Therefore, it could not prevent U.S. nuclear retaliation should China strike the United States first.[66]

Still, China does have capabilities that could threaten the physical security of the United States and its territories to a limited degree. Although China is unlikely to use these capabilities in an unprovoked attack on the United States, it could employ them the context of a wider

---

[61] The PLA Navy also does not have the supporting infrastructure in place for sustained operations overseas, including limited logistics and sealift capabilities. See Office of the Secretary of Defense, 2021, pp. 81–86, 130–131; and Joel Wuthnow, Phillip C. Saunders, and Ian Burns McCaslin, *PLA Overseas Operations in 2035: Inching Toward a Global Combat Capability*, Washington, D.C.: Institute for National Strategic Studies, National Defense University, Strategic Forum No. 309, May 2021, p. 14.

[62] Eugene Gholz, interview with the authors, video call, April 30, 2021. For the restraint view, see Gholz, Press, and Sapolsky, 1997; and Posen, 2014.

[63] Hans M. Kristensen and Robert S. Norris, "United States Nuclear Forces, 2017," *Bulletin of the Atomic Scientists*, Vol. 73, No. 1, 2017, p. 48; Office of the Secretary of Defense, 2020, p. viii; Office of the Secretary of Defense, 2021, pp. 90–94.

[64] Office of the Secretary of Defense, 2021; Ronald O'Rourke, *China Naval Modernization: Implications for U.S. Navy Capabilities—Background and Issues for Congress*, Washington, D.C.: Congressional Research Service, September 9, 2021b, p. 4.

[65] Office of the Secretary of Defense, 2021, p. 80.

[66] China only recently (in February 2021) conducted a successful first test of its ground-based antiballistic missile capabilities against a midcourse IRBM target (Liu Xuanzun, "China Conducts Mid-Course Antiballistic Missile Test, System 'Becomes More Mature, Reliable,'" *Global Times*, last updated February 5, 2021).

war. China is building some military capabilities, especially long-range bombers and missiles, that can reach Hawaii and U.S. territories, such as Guam. China has fielded increasing numbers of H-6K bombers, which can carry land-attack cruise missiles (LACMs) and can target territory 2,000 mi away from China. This provides the PLA with a precision strike capability that can reach Guam and the Northern Marianas from mainland China and the South China Sea, and it could also threaten these islands with cruise missiles launched by submarines.[67] A maritime variant of this bomber, the H-6J, carries anti-ship cruise missiles (ASCMs) that can attack naval vessels within the same range.[68] China is developing the stealthy H-20 long-range strategic bomber, which could launch standoff missile attacks against Hawaii in the future,[69] and the PLA is augmenting its arsenal of conventional precision-strike ballistic missiles that could reach Guam and Hawaii.[70]

The PLA Rocket Force (PLARF) possesses an estimated 100 ICBMs that have a range of greater than 5,500 km and could reach Hawaii and potentially Alaska.[71] The PLARF has continued to develop and deploy increasing numbers of road-mobile ICBMs that can target most of the continental United States.[72] China is also modernizing its submarine fleet, including developing nuclear-powered ballistic missile submarines (SSBNs) to augment China's land-based nuclear deterrent. Most of China's SSBNs are armed with the JL-2 SLBM, which, for the first time, gives the country the capability to attack the United States and its territories with nuclear weapons by sea.[73] According to DoD's 2021 report on China's military power, the range limitations of the JL-2 would require China's SSBNs "to operate in areas north and

---

[67] Liu Xuanzun, "China's H-6K Bomber Expected to Be Armed with Hypersonic," *Global Times*, August 6, 2019. China has deployed these bombers to Woody Island in the South China Sea, which puts both Guam and northern Australia within range (Asia Maritime Transparency Initiative, "China Lands First Bomber on South China Sea Island," May 18, 2018).

[68] Franz-Stefan Gady, "China's Navy Deploys New H-6J Anti-Ship Cruise Missile-Carrying Bombers," *The Diplomat*, October 12, 2018; Office of the Secretary of Defense, 2020, p. 51; Office of the Secretary of Defense, 2021, p. 81.

[69] Nathan Beauchamp-Mustafaga, "Bomber Strike Packages with Chinese Characteristics," in Joel Wuthnow, Arthur S. Ding, Phillip C. Saunders, Andrew Scobell, and Andrew N. D. Yang, eds., *The PLA Beyond Borders: Chinese Military Operations in Regional and Global Context*, Washington, D.C.: National Defense University Press, 2021, p. 225. The H-20 would likely have a range of 8,500 km and could carry both conventional and nuclear missiles.

[70] Office of the Secretary of Defense, 2020, p. 166. DoD projects that the "number of warheads on the PRC's land-based ICBMs capable of threatening the United States is expected to grow to roughly 200 in the next five years," partly because China is developing multiple independently targetable reentry vehicle (MIRV) systems (Office of the Secretary of Defense, 2021, pp. 60–61).

[71] Office of the Secretary of Defense, 2021, p. 163.

[72] Defense Intelligence Ballistic Missile Analysis Committee, *Ballistic and Cruise Missile Threat*, Wright-Patterson Air Force Base, Ohio: National Air and Space Intelligence Center, 2020, pp. 26–27. The PLARF is also expanding its inventory of DF-26 IRBMs, which are nuclear capable and can reach Guam (Office of the Secretary of Defense, 2021, p. 60).

[73] Zhao, 2020.

east of Hawaii if the PRC seeks to target the east coast of the United States."[74] Chinese SSBNs operating in this area would be more vulnerable to U.S. anti-submarine warfare than SSBNs operating in areas closer to the Chinese coast.[75] China has also developed its third-generation JL-3 SLBM, which has an estimated range of more than 9,000 km and could allow the PLA to target parts of the United States from China's littoral waters.[76]

Finally, China is developing cyber capabilities that could threaten the U.S. homeland by targeting U.S. defense systems, civilian infrastructure, or economic institutions.[77] China already employs some cyber capabilities during peacetime. For example, China has used its cyber capabilities to disseminate false information and harvest data from other countries' government and commercial systems.[78] The PLA's recent reform efforts have focused on further integrating cyber, space, and electronic warfare capabilities that it can use to gain an information advantage in a conflict, as well as to threaten U.S. communications, navigation, and intelligence capabilities.[79] Although the PLA would primarily use these in a regional conflict, the PLA's integration and networking of cyber capabilities could enable it to target an adversary's information systems outside the region.[80] The United States has some counters to Chinese cyber capabilities, but U.S. defense planners generally acknowledge that China will have some ability to degrade civilian and military systems through cyberattacks should a conflict occur.[81]

---

[74] Office of the Secretary of Defense, 2021, p. 91.

[75] Office of the Secretary of Defense, 2021, p. 91.

[76] Hans M. Kristensen and Matt Korda, "Chinese Nuclear Forces, 2019," *Bulletin of the Atomic Scientists*, Vol. 75, No. 4, 2019; Office of the Secretary of Defense, 2021.

[77] Office of the Director of National Intelligence, 2021, p. 8; Office of the Secretary of Defense, 2021.

[78] Chinese military literature discusses the use of cyber capabilities to degrade or shape an adversary's decisionmaking by injecting false or confusing information, accessing information systems, and controlling or destroying data (Office of the Secretary of Defense, 2020, p. 74). For a discussion of China's use of cyber capabilities in peacetime and wartime, see Dean Cheng, *Cyber Dragon: Inside China's Information Warfare and Cyber Operations*, Santa Barbara, Calif.: Praeger, 2016.

[79] The PLA's Strategic Support Force is the primary institution that integrates these capabilities (John Costello and Joe McReynolds, "China's Strategic Support Force: A Force for a New Era," in Phillip C. Saunders, Arthur S. Ding, Andrew Scobell, Andrew N. D. Yang, and Joel Wuthnow, eds., *Chairman Xi Remakes the PLA: Assessing Chinese Military Reforms*, Washington, D.C.: National Defense University Press, 2019; Office of the Secretary of Defense, 2021).

[80] The PLA views the use of cyber capabilities as critical to gaining information dominance prior to and during a conflict. China would combine some of these efforts with its information operations and potentially direct them against targets in the U.S. homeland (Dean Cheng, "Getting to Where the PLA Needs to Be," testimony presented before U.S.-China Economic and Security Review Commission, Washington, D.C., June 20, 2019).

[81] For an overview of the threat that China's cyber activities pose, see International Institute for Strategic Studies, "Chapter Five: China's Cyber Power in a New Era," *Asia Pacific Regional Security Assessment 2019*, Washington, D.C., 2019.

Restrainers do not believe that these military developments constitute a serious threat to the continental United States. China's conventional long-range precision strike capabilities are still at a relatively early stage of development, and the United States has some ability through missile defense, naval, and air capabilities to counter threats from China's missiles against the U.S. homeland. Moreover, the United States has nuclear capabilities that could survive a Chinese first strike. Restrainers argue that this secure second-strike capability should deter nuclear attacks on the U.S. homeland, along with other large-scale attacks if these became feasible. It is not clear how much Chinese power-projection and long-range strike capabilities would need to develop to change restrainers' assessment or at what point in the growth of Chinese capabilities they would favor changing U.S. posture in response.

Threats to Regional U.S. Military Access and Trade

Defense analysts discuss the threat that China could pose to the U.S. ability to move military forces and protect trade in two areas: (1) within the first island chain and (2) from the first island chain to the second island chain and beyond (see Figure 2.1). China has invested in anti-access/area denial (A2/AD) capabilities that increasingly put U.S. forces and commercial vessels at potential risk within the first island chain.[82] However, restrainers generally would not fight to prevent China from restricting U.S. trade and operations there.

China is also developing the capabilities to sustain maritime and air operations beyond the first island chain, where restrainers see a greater U.S. interest in freedom of navigation. The PLA Navy (PLAN) is building a modernized fleet that includes surface combatants, submarines, amphibious warfare ships, and aircraft carriers, along with naval aviation forces, which could target and disrupt U.S. operations beyond the first island chain in a conflict. China currently fields anti-ship ballistic missile (ASBM) versions of its medium-range ballistic missiles (MRBMs) and IRBMs that can target moving ships if they have targeting information from a mix of systems, including satellites, over-the-horizon radars located on the mainland, and aircraft. The DF-21D ASBM has a range of approximately 1,500 km, and the DF-26 variant's range is around 4,000 km.[83] To threaten U.S. forces out to the second island chain, the PLA could also use ground-based ballistic and cruise missile forces in tandem with air- and sea-launched ASCMs and LACMs, although the PLA currently has limited long-range targeting capability for these missiles against mobile targets.[84]

---

[82] Over the past 15 years, the PLA has focused on developing forces and capabilities to prevent uncontested access to China's air and maritime approaches in the East China Sea, South China Sea, and Yellow Sea. These A2/AD capabilities are meant to prevent U.S. access to and contest freedom of movement within the Indo-Pacific region (Defense Intelligence Ballistic Missile Analysis Committee, 2020, pp. 21, 25; Office of the Secretary of Defense, 2021, p. 77; O'Rourke, 2021b, pp. 16, 24–25).

[83] China reportedly tested these missiles in 2020 and successfully hit a moving ship in the South China Sea (Andrew Erickson, "China's DF-21D and DF-26B ASBMs: Is the U.S. Military Ready?" *RealClearDefense*, November 16, 2020; Office of the Secretary of Defense, 2021, pp. 61, 78).

[84] Office of the Secretary of Defense, 2020, p. 62; Office of the Secretary of Defense, 2021, pp. 51, 77–78; O'Rourke, 2021b, pp. 4, 48.

Despite these improvements, the PLA would still face challenges in conducting air and naval operations beyond the first island chain, particularly during conflict, because it does not yet possess a logistics system that can sustain forces farther from China's periphery for long periods.[85] As a result, the PLA might be able to disrupt U.S. access to the region intermittently, but it could not yet exercise its own control of distant SLOCs outright. Another constraint is China's command, control, communications, computers, and ISR (C4ISR) infrastructure to support military operations, which the PLA is working to improve but which remains limited for forces past the first island chain.[86] That said, in the next decade, China will possess some capabilities to target U.S. forces and disrupt shipping in a limited manner out to the second island chain if it wishes to do so.[87] The PLA could deploy flotillas of surface ships with anti-ship missiles and surface-to-air missiles (SAMs) accompanied by submarine patrols to harass and threaten U.S. forces and merchant shipping, although it would likely face limitations in the scale of forces that it could deploy and its ability to sustain operations for a long period (e.g., many months) without increased access to regional ports for resupply. Despite potentially being able to disrupt U.S. forces and shipping out to the second island chain, China will likely lack the ability to fully deny U.S. military or commercial access in this area over the next decade.

Threats to Japan

Advocates of restraint do not see significant threats from China to Japan's survival as an independent state.[88] They contend that Japan has substantial military capability to defend its home islands,[89] especially given the geographic advantage that defenders have against long-distance amphibious assaults and Japan's incentives to invest more heavily in self-defense if the United States were to scale back its security guarantees. Restrainers also generally consider nationalism to be a powerful motivating force, and they expect the Japanese people to

---

[85] For an overview of the challenges that the PLA faces in building a logistics system that can support forces overseas, see LeighAnn Luce and Erin Richter, "Handling Logistics in a Reformed PLA: The Long March Toward Jointness," in Phillip C. Saunders, Arthur S. Ding, Andrew Scobell, Andrew N. D. Yang, and Joel Wuthnow, eds., *Chairman Xi Remakes the PLA: Assessing Chinese Military Reforms*, Washington D.C.: National Defense University Press, 2019.

[86] Kristen Gunness, "The PLA's Expeditionary Force: Capabilities and Trends," in Joel Wuthnow, Arthur S. Ding, Phillip C. Saunders, Andrew Scobell, and Andrew N. D. Yang, eds., *The PLA Beyond Borders: Chinese Military Operations in Regional and Global Context*, Washington, D.C.: National Defense University Press, 2021, pp. 32–34; Office of the Secretary of Defense, 2021, pp. 51, 78, 86–87.

[87] For a discussion of China's naval reforms and trends, see Ian Burns McCaslin and Andrew S. Erickson, "The Impact of Xi-Era Reforms on the Chinese Navy," in Phillip C. Saunders, Arthur S. Ding, Andrew Scobell, Andrew N. D. Yang, and Joel Wuthnow, eds., *Chairman Xi Remakes the PLA: Assessing Chinese Military Reforms*, Washington, D.C.: National Defense University Press, 2019; and Office of the Secretary of Defense, 2021, p. 77.

[88] Jasen J. Castillo, interview with the authors, video call, May 3, 2021.

[89] Japan does not use the term *military* when referring to its self-defense forces. However, these forces have what are commonly understood to be military capabilities, so we apply that term to them.

have a strong will to fight if the conquest of Japan is at stake. However, these strategists do note the possibility of a Chinese coercive campaign against Japan.[90] There are ongoing disputes between China and Japan (most notably, control of the Senkaku/Diaoyu Islands, as we discuss in Chapter Three) that could plausibly escalate into a military confrontation in which China could bring its substantial military capabilities to bear against Japan. Moreover, as we discuss in Chapter Four, China's long-term maritime ambitions and the geography of the region mean that the Ryukyu island chain could become another plausible flashpoint. Advocates of restraint have not carefully analyzed the threat that China poses to Japan's military power or to the Ryukyus.[91]

Overall, the most likely military threat from China, should it choose to attack Japan, would be from missile strikes against key military infrastructure (such as runways, bases, and air and missile defenses) followed by attacks from aircraft, surface ships, and submarines to disable Japan's naval and air assets. Such an attack could come from an escalating dispute over the Senkaku Islands or the Ryukyu Islands or from Japan's involvement in a war over Taiwan. Chinese military capabilities that could target Japan's territory or its naval and air forces include the PLA's large and growing arsenal of precision strike missiles, such as ASBMs, MRBMs, and LACMs.[92] The PLAN is upgrading and deploying surface combatants with modern air defenses and longer-range ASCMs.[93] While the PLA has had some challenges in fielding the ISR required for striking mobile targets with these missiles, the PLAN is seeking to solve this issue by investing in over-the-horizon targeting capabilities, such as more and better satellites.[94] In addition to anti-ship missile systems, the PLAN is modernizing its submarine force.[95] China could use these capabilities, particularly its land-attack and anti-ship missiles, to threaten or significantly degrade Japan's naval forces in a conflict.

The PLAN has expanded its amphibious capabilities, which are central to China's ability to project military force during a conflict. The PLAN Marine Corps is the PLAN's land

---

[90] Jasen J. Castillo, interview with the authors, video call, May 3, 2021; Eugene Gholz, interview with the authors, video call, April 30, 2021; Gholz, Friedman, and Gjoza, 2020, p. 181; Gholz, Press, and Sapolsky, 1997, pp. 20–22; Posen, 2014, pp. 99–100.

[91] Earlier assessments assumed that Japanese air and naval forces had large quantitative and qualitative advantages against potential Chinese attacks (Gholz, Press, and Sapolsky, 1997, p. 21). More-recent assessments have argued that the Japanese navy retains some qualitative advantages over the PLA and that it should continue to make greater investments in mobile anti-access systems for defending its territory (Gholz, Friedman, and Gjoza, 2020). Another study acknowledged that China could attempt an invasion of the Ryukyus but did not analyze this scenario other than mentioning that it would strengthen China's power-projection capabilities by removing a geographic barrier to the PLA's access to the Pacific (Posen, 2014, p. 99).

[92] Office of the Secretary of Defense, 2020, p. 72; Office of the Secretary of Defense, 2021, pp. 61, 77–78.

[93] Office of the Secretary of Defense, 2021, pp. 49–50, 78.

[94] Office of the Secretary of Defense, 2020, p. 46; Office of the Secretary of Defense, 2021, p. 51.

[95] Office of the Secretary of Defense, 2021, p. 49; Kristen Gunness, "The China Dream in the Near Seas," in Roy Kamphausen, David Lai, and Tiffany Ma, eds., *Securing the China Dream: The PLA's Role in a Time of Reform and Change*, Seattle, Wash.: National Bureau of Asian Research, 2020, pp. 84–86.

combat arm. Its primary regional mission is to conduct amphibious assault in a regional contingency in conjunction with other PLA ground forces, and this capability would be critical in any attempts to seize Japanese territory.[96] However, while the PLA's amphibious capabilities are improving, issues of command and control and cross-service coordination during joint operations, in addition to a newly restructured PLAN Marine Corps and a lack of training in a joint environment, would likely hinder the PLA's capabilities in a large-scale amphibious operation, at least in the near future.[97]

Japan does have substantial defense capabilities against other aspects of a Chinese attack. Japan's ballistic missile defense system includes Aegis-equipped destroyers in the Japan Maritime Self-Defense Force's (JMSDF's) and Japan Air Self-Defense Force's (JASDF's) Patriot Advanced Capability-3 interceptors that can counter limited numbers of missiles closer to their targets.[98] It is not clear how many interceptors Japan has or how easily a large-scale Chinese attack could overwhelm these systems. In addition, Japan is investing in standoff missile capabilities that could enhance its air and missile defenses by holding PLA forces at risk at greater range.[99] In addition, the JMSDF has a fleet of modern destroyers and submarines with upgraded ASW capabilities that it can deploy to defend the Japanese coastline and threaten Chinese forces that enter Japan's territorial waters.[100]

Despite these improvements, the gap between China's and Japan's military capabilities is growing and will continue to do so absent substantial efforts by Japan to reverse these trends by investing more in its armed forces—and likely will continue to do so to a lesser degree even if Japan does devote greater resources to defense, given the size and economic disparity between the two countries. China's naval advancements over the past decade have outpaced those of the JMSDF, both qualitatively and quantitatively. In terms of size, the PLAN has 350 ships and is growing while the JMSDF's force is significantly smaller, at 135 ships.[101] Table 2.3 compares the numbers of key ships and aircraft in China's and Japan's navies and air forces.

Beyond the number of ships, the PLAN is upgrading its anti-air and anti-surface warfare capabilities, including a large arsenal of ship-based ASCMs that outrange those of the

---

[96] Gunness, 2021, pp. 23–40.

[97] As we discuss in the following chapters, amphibious operations would also face challenges related to protecting ships headed toward a target. These challenges would similarly apply to an invasion of Taiwan, although the much longer distances involved in an assault on Japanese territory would greatly magnify many of them (Office of the Secretary of Defense, 2020, p. 48; Office of the Secretary of Defense, 2021, pp. 52–120).

[98] Japan Ministry of Defense, "Part III: Three Pillars of Japan's Defense," *Defense of Japan 2020*, Tokyo, 2020b.

[99] Jeffrey W. Hornung, *Japan's Potential Contributions in an East China Sea Contingency*, Santa Monica, Calif.: RAND Corporation, RR-A314-1, 2020a, p. 66.

[100] Tim Fish, "Japan Maritime Self-Defense Force Expanding as Tokyo Takes New Approach to Maritime Security," USNI News, May 29, 2019.

[101] Toshi Yoshihara, "How China Has Overtaken Japan in Naval Power and Why It Matters," Center for International Maritime Security, June 22, 2020b.

JMSDF, posing a threat to Japan's ability to defend itself against a maritime attack.[102] The JMSDF's current ASW capability is somewhat better than the PLAN's, which would assist Japan in defending its coastal waters. However, the PLAN is investing in more-robust ASW capabilities, although the improvements to date have been modest.[103]

China's air force and its naval aviation capabilities make up the largest aviation force in the Asia-Pacific, with more than 2,000 fixed-wing combat aircraft, according to DoD estimates.[104] By comparison, the JASDF and JMSDF have less than one-fourth as many,[105] and these aircraft and the supporting air base infrastructure would be vulnerable to attack by Chinese missiles. Raw numbers do not tell the whole story. In general, the PLA Air Force (PLAAF) is fielding fourth-generation fighters while the JASDF is investing in more-advanced

TABLE 2.3

China's and Japan's Major Naval Combatants and Combat Aircraft, Early 2021

Ships or Aircraft	China	Japan
Aircraft carriers	2	–
Helicopter carriers	–	4[a]
Cruisers and destroyers	32	41
Frigates and corvettes	101	6
Amphibious transport docks	6	3
Attack submarines (nuclear)	9	–
Attack submarines (conventional)	56	22
Maritime patrol aircraft	16+	72
Bombers	209	–
Fighter and attack aircraft	1,820	335

SOURCE: International Institute for Strategic Studies, "Asia," *Military Balance*, Vol. 121, No. 1, 2021a, pp. 251–255, 271–273.
NOTES: Totals shown are for aircraft counted as operational.
[a] In 2018, the Japanese government confirmed that it will convert two helicopter carriers into light aircraft carriers.

---

[102] For a description of JMSDF capabilities and challenges, see Jeffrey W. Hornung and Scott W. Harold, "Japan's Potential Acquisition of Ground-Launched Land-Attack Missiles: Implications for the U.S.-Japan Alliance," *War on the Rocks*, September 9, 2021, pp. 45–54.

[103] Defense Intelligence Agency, *China Military Power: Modernizing a Force to Fight and Win*, Washington, D.C., 2019, p. 69; Office of the Secretary of Defense, 2021, pp. 49–50.

[104] Office of the Secretary of Defense, 2021, p. 55.

[105] International Institute for Strategic Studies, 2021a, pp. 253–255, 272–273.

aviation platforms, including F-35s, which will enhance Japan's air-to-air and air-to-surface capabilities; upgrading its F-15s; and developing an F-X stealth fighter, which, after a series of program delays, the JASDF now plans to begin fielding by 2035.[106] However, China is also beginning to deploy fifth-generation fighters, so Japan's ability to compensate for its smaller number of aircraft with qualitative advantages may be diminishing.[107]

As with threats to the U.S. homeland, China's cyber capabilities could threaten Japan. China has previously launched cyber intrusions against Japanese industry and government organizations to gather data on defense policies and plans.[108] China's offensive cyber capabilities could also target Japanese ISR and military systems, as well as infrastructure. Although Japan and the United States have worked together on cybersecurity, there are still gaps in Japan's ability to respond to a significant Chinese cyberattack should one occur.[109]

Given the PLA's growing air, missile, naval, and cyber capabilities compared with Japan's countermeasures, China could plausibly try to coerce Japan with an air, missile, and cyber campaign or a blockade, which we consider in greater detail in Chapter Three. China could also contest Japan's control of the Ryukyu Islands given that it would use similar naval, air, and amphibious capabilities to those it has developed for a regional contingency within the first island chain and Japan currently has minimal defenses on at least some of the islands.[110] As we discuss in Chapter Four, if China were to gain control of Taiwan, the PLA would have an increased ability to project power against the Ryukyus. In short, in the next decade, there is at least a plausible threat—due to China's capability to launch coercive air, missile, and cyberattacks or attempt a blockade—to restrainers' objectives of maintaining Japan's foreign policy independence and ensuring that the Ryukyu Islands remain under Japanese control.

---

[106] Hornung, 2020a, p. 36. See also Defense Security Cooperation Agency, "Japan F-35 Joint Strike Fighter Aircraft," news release, Washington, D.C., July 9, 2020; and Mike Yeo, "Japan Names Contractor to Build Its Future Fighter Jet," Yahoo! October 30, 2020.

[107] DoD reports that 800 of the PLA's 1,800 fighters are fourth-generation aircraft and that the PLA "probably will become a majority fourth-generation force within the next several years" (Office of the Secretary of Defense, 2021, p. 55). It has still only "operationally fielded limited numbers of its new J-20" fifth-generation aircraft (p. 55).

[108] Center for Strategic and International Studies, "Significant Cyber Incidents Since 2006," incidents list, undated.

[109] James Andrew Lewis, *U.S.-Japan Cooperation in Cybersecurity*, Washington, D.C.: Center for Strategic and International Studies, November 2015, pp. 10–11.

[110] China's regional contingencies within the first island chain include an East China Sea (Japan) conflict and a Taiwan conflict. For a discussion of Japan's defense strategy and capabilities, see Hornung and Harold, 2021. For insight into the Japan Self-Defense Force's limitations in defending the Ryukyus and Senkakus/Diaoyus from Chinese attack, see Masafumi Iida, *China's Security Threats and Japan's Responses*, Washington, D.C.: Center for Strategic and International Studies, 2021.

Threats to South Korea

Advocates of restraint and other analysts typically focus on the threat that North Korea poses to South Korea.[111] But our focus here is on the threat that China poses, which is something that advocates of restraint have not addressed explicitly. However, restrainers have implied that South Korea could be vulnerable to Chinese coercion. China could use many of the same military capabilities—such as ballistic missiles and naval forces—against South Korea that it could use against Japan. Whereas China and Japan have ongoing territorial disputes, the potential causes of a major military conflict between China and South Korea are less obvious. China's primary concern with respect to the Korean Peninsula is North Korea, where it fears a collapse of the government could lead to severe instability and a large refugee flow that could spill into China. Were that to occur, China could plausibly send the PLA into North Korea to help maintain stability or secure North Korean nuclear facilities.[112] Given China's objective of restoring stability in North Korea, Beijing would likely keep its forces away from the South Korean border to minimize the risk of armed conflict with South Korea. China's actions in a North Korea scenario are unlikely to threaten South Korean independence, so we did not include countering Chinese threats to South Korea as a military mission that restrainers would prioritize.

Military Missions

Where restrainers' regional objectives and current or potential threats intersect, there are military missions that would guide DoD planning under a grand strategy of restraint. This section outlines a set of military missions focusing on China in the Asia-Pacific that appear to reflect the central concerns of more-restrained grand strategies.

This project focuses on U.S. policy choices in the coming decade, but, in some cases, the United States might need to adjust its policies within the next ten years even if there is not a clear threat within the same time frame. For example, it might need to build or maintain certain forces, bases, or security relationships in the 2020s to prepare for potential threats in the mid-to-late 2030s. This is because development and procurement timelines for modern

---

[111] Flexible and defensive restrainers argue that, because South Korea can defend itself against a North Korean invasion, a gradual withdrawal of U.S. forces from the Korean Peninsula is preferable. For example, Posen argues that the geography of the peninsula makes defense against invasion easier than offense, South Korea has qualitatively better military forces, and South Korea has the wealth to improve its capabilities if the United States withdraws (Posen, 2014, p. 105). Restrainers have not, however, said much about South Korea's ability to respond to threats short of conquest posed by North Korea (Priebe et al., 2021).

[112] For a discussion of China's North Korea strategy, see Andrew Scobell, "China and North Korea: Bolstering a Buffer or Hunkering Down in Northeast Asia?" testimony presented before the U.S.-China Economic and Security Review Commission on June 8, 2017, Santa Monica, Calif.: RAND Corporation, CT-477, 2017. See also Oriana Skylar Mastro, "Conflict and Chaos on the Korean Peninsula: Can China's Military Help Secure North Korea's Nuclear Weapons?" *International Security*, Vol. 43, No. 2, Fall 2018.

equipment are long, and the expertise of professional military personnel is similarly something that takes time to develop.

As we noted earlier, there are variations among advocates of restraint regarding regional objectives. Table 2.4 reflects the same three ideal-type variations within the restraint community that we introduced in Chapter One. In a defensive restraint approach, the United States would limit its principal military efforts to maintaining a capability to deal with maritime, air, and cyber threats to the United States and its territory. Strategists in this camp prefer to have the capability to maintain U.S. maritime access to the high seas but would not pay a high price to do so.

Those in the flexible restraint camp agree that the United States is currently highly secure but contend that it should have greater insurance against the possibility that more-significant threats might arise in the future because the international environment is inherently uncertain. Retaining a strong U.S. military relative to potential adversaries' militaries constitutes a hedge against future insecurity. That said, flexible restrainers want a smaller and less active military than the United States currently has. In this formulation, the United States would place greater emphasis on maintaining its ability to project power in key maritime areas and to defend Japan. However, whether the United States would actually fight in these situations would depend on the context, especially the anticipated costs and risks of fighting versus military inaction.

The final ideal type, counterhegemonic restraint, captures the view among some restrainers that preventing China from becoming a regional hegemon is a vital U.S. interest that warrants serious attention in the near term. They are more willing to fight to prevent China's power from expanding, to prevent the loss or weakening of regional powers that stand in the way of China's rise, and to sustain U.S. access to key areas of the Asia-Pacific theater.[113]

The remainder of this section describes military missions that at least some advocates of restraint would support.

Deter and Defend Against Chinese Attacks on the United States and U.S. Territory

Air, cyber, and missile attacks represent the most significant threat that China could pose to the United States and its territories. Advocates of restraint propose several approaches to addressing this threat. The first is deterrence. Maintaining the conventional and nuclear capability to retaliate against China should dissuade China from air and missile attacks in many circumstances. Politically, advocates of restraint would also seek to avoid situations

---

[113] However, few, if any, restrainers—even in this camp—would support the preventive use of military force against China to impede its economic rise. This is partly a definitional issue because an advocate of preventive war would be calling for a less rather than more restrained policy relative to the current U.S. approach. It also reflects a realist perspective that, while states can contain a rival, history suggests that trying to use military force to override the economic and political drivers of national growth tends to be expensive and unsuccessful, even when dealing with non–nuclear-armed challengers that are far smaller than China.

TABLE 2.4

Military Missions to Address Threats from China Under Alternative Visions of Restraint

Objective	Defensive Restraint	Flexible Restraint	Counter-hegemonic Restraint	Recent U.S. Grand Strategy
Secure the United States and U.S. territories against major air, missile, or cyberattacks.	■	■	■	■
Prevent China from denying U.S. naval and trade access to the Pacific outside the first island chain.	▨	■	■	■
Prevent a successful Chinese blockade or coercive bombardment of Japan.	□	■	■	■
Prevent China from severely weakening Japan's air or naval power.	□	▨	■	■
Prevent China from seizing Okinawa or other islands in the Ryukyus.	□	▨	■	■
Maintain the ability to conduct a sustained distant blockade of China.	□	▨	■	■
Prevent China from seizing the Senkaku/Diaoyu Islands.	□	□	▨	■
Prevent China from seizing Taiwan.	□	□	▨	■
Prevent China from denying friendly military and commercial access inside the first island chain.	□	□	▨	■

NOTES: Dark blue cells indicate vital U.S. security interests—i.e., U.S. forces should be prepared to carry out the mission if needed. Lighter blue cells indicate that the ability to execute the mission is desirable if success appears feasible at a reasonable cost. Beige cells indicate that the strategy does not recommend investing in the ability to execute the mission. Restrainers often call for a multiyear transition from current U.S. commitments to these preferred outcomes. The list of objectives for recent U.S. grand strategy is not comprehensive. The "recent U.S. grand strategy" column also represents strategies that involve restraint in other regions but not in the Asia-Pacific.

that could give China incentives to attack the United States, such as a war between the two countries over another issue, most obviously Taiwan.[114]

Because war over a vital interest would remain possible, restrainers still support maintaining U.S. air defenses because of current Russian and future Chinese long-range strike capabilities. However, advocates of restraint are skeptical about the value of national missile defense systems given their costs relative to their effectiveness, and they do not believe that investment in strategic defense can eliminate U.S. vulnerability in a major nuclear exchange.[115] Cyber defenses during war and peace would also remain a priority for restrainers.

---

[114] Carpenter and Gomez, 2016; Posen, 2014, p. 96; Joshua Shifrinson, "The Rise of China, Balance of Power Theory and US National Security: Reasons for Optimism?" *Journal of Strategic Studies*, Vol. 43, No. 2, 2020.

[115] Eugene Gholz, interview with the authors, video call, April 30, 2021.

Preserve the U.S. Ability to Operate in Areas of the Pacific Outside the First Island Chain

To preserve U.S. trade and military access in the areas outside the first island chain, including the Philippine Sea and the Pacific Ocean, the United States would want to maintain the capability to thwart a Chinese naval, air, and missile offensive in these waters. This capability would also allow the United States to protect against a Chinese attack on trade bound for the United States or U.S. military vessels transiting to other regions.

To thwart a Chinese submarine offensive outside the first island chain, the United States would rely on ASW operations to track and restrict the movement of Chinese submarines. This would involve continued investment in attack submarines, ASW-capable surface ships, maritime patrol aircraft (MPA), ocean surveillance ships, and the U.S. and allied undersea sound surveillance network.[116] Countering Chinese air and missile threats against U.S. and allied naval forces or merchant shipping would involve U.S. Navy surface combatants conducting convoy escort missions, and land- or carrier-based airpower (or both) defending against air and cruise missile attacks and launching attacks against enemy surface vessels.[117]

An increasing concern for U.S. naval forces is countering China's kill chain that enables ASBM and long-range ASCM attacks against U.S. ships. The U.S. response could involve kinetic, cyber, or electronic attacks against over-the-horizon radars in China, aircraft, satellites, or the command, control, and communications links that connect them.[118] However, restrainers are wary of launching attacks against the homelands of nuclear-armed enemies because of escalation concerns, so they might instead accept the risk that these systems pose to shipping.

Preserve the U.S. Ability to Conduct a Distant Blockade of China

Some advocates of restraint support maintaining the capability to conduct a distant blockade of China.[119] They do so even though they acknowledge that blockades are not effective instruments in all cases. Blockades work slowly by imposing cumulative costs on the

---

[116] Owen R. Coté, Jr., *Assessing the Undersea Balance Between the U.S. and China*, Cambridge, Mass.: MIT Security Studies Program, SSP Working Paper, 2011; Tong Zhao, *Tides of Change: U.S. Anti-Submarine Warfare and Its Impact*, Washington, D.C.: Carnegie-Tsinghua Center for Global Policy, 2018.

[117] U.S. Navy, U.S. Marine Corps, and U.S. Coast Guard, 2020, pp. 13–14.

[118] Stephen Biddle and Ivan Oelrich, "Future Warfare in the Western Pacific: Chinese Antiaccess/Area Denial, U.S. AirSea Battle, and Command of the Commons in East Asia," *International Security*, Vol. 41, No. 1, 2016.

[119] Jennifer Lind, "Keep, Toss, or Fix? Assessing US Alliance in East Asia," in Jeremi Suri and Benjamin Valentino, eds., *Sustainable Security: Rethinking American National Security Strategy*, Oxford: Oxford University Press, 2016, pp. 298–299, 313–314; Posen, 2014, pp. 141–142; Benjamin Schwarz and Christopher Layne, "A New Grand Strategy," *The Atlantic*, January 2002; Joshua Shifrinson, "Should the United States Fear China's Rise?" *Washington Quarterly*, Vol. 41, No. 4, 2019, p. 77. Not all advocates of restraint agree. For example, Ashford argues that a blockade could be quite escalatory (Emma Ashford, interview with the authors, video call, August 25, 2021).

enemy. Because states have ways to weather blockades, such as rationing goods and substituting for materials in short supply, blockades are unlikely to be effective in cases in which an adversary has vital interests at stake and is willing to pay a high price to achieve its goals.[120] This means that a U.S. blockade would be very unlikely to convince China to abandon an ongoing invasion of Taiwan if Chinese leaders believed the invasion was likely to succeed. Posen notes that a blockade is "not a magic bullet" and that costs "of this kind probably cannot 'win' a victory in a major dispute. But the threat may deter limited aggression, increase the odds that the initiator may suffer a net loss in a large conflict, or help bring a conflict to a negotiated conclusion."[121]

There are still several reasons that restrainers might want to retain the capability to conduct a distant blockade of the major maritime choke points through which China's shipping passes. First, compared with strategies involving U.S. strikes on the Chinese mainland or large-scale combat between U.S. and Chinese forces, a distant blockade may reduce the risk of escalation to a wider conflict or nuclear use.[122] China has limited power-projection capabilities, so, although a distant blockade might involve some fighting between the two sides, it would be more limited than it would be if the United States were to pursue a military campaign closer to China. Moreover, operating beyond the range of most PLA capabilities would reduce the temptation for the United States to protect its forces by attacking military targets on the Chinese mainland. However, a blockade that was effective enough to cripple the Chinese economy would be threatening a core interest of the Chinese Communist Party, so it could generate considerable escalatory pressures for political reasons even if the United States minimized the scope of the military campaign to enforce the blockade. This would be especially likely if Chinese leaders believed that economic hardship could imperil the regime's survival by fueling internal instability.

The second reason a distant blockade might be an appealing option is that it plays to U.S. strengths and Chinese vulnerabilities. The U.S. Navy remains far ahead of any other country's navy on the open oceans. At the same time, China's oceanic trade has to pass through a small number of maritime choke points that make it vulnerable to disruption, as we discuss

---

[120] Mancur Olson, Jr., *The Economics of the Wartime Shortage: A History of British Food Supplies in the Napoleonic War and in World Wars I and II*, Durham, N.C.: Duke University Press, 1963.

[121] Posen, 2014, pp. 141–142. Similarly, Mearsheimer argues that the impact of blockades "is usually limited" because great powers can become proficient at "recycling, stockpiling, and substitution" and redirecting public grievances toward the enemy rather than the government (Mearsheimer, 2001, pp. 94–96).

[122] Fiona S. Cunningham, "The Maritime Rung on the Escalation Ladder: Naval Blockades in a US-China Conflict," *Security Studies*, Vol. 29, No. 4, 2020; T. X. Hammes, *Offshore Control: A Proposed Strategy for an Unlikely Conflict*, Washington, D.C.: Institute for National Strategic Studies, National Defense University, No. 278, June 2012. The United States could also impose a close blockade to threaten merchant shipping in China's littoral waters, but this would place U.S. forces at greater risk and would increase the potential for escalation. See Gabriel B. Collins and William S. Murray, "No Oil for the Lamps of China?" *Naval War College Review*, Vol. 61, No. 2, Spring 2008; and Sean Mirski, "Stranglehold: The Context, Conduct and Consequences of an American Naval Blockade of China," *Journal of Strategic Studies*, Vol. 36, No. 3, 2013.

in Chapter Five.[123] China is aware of this vulnerability and has taken steps to reduce it, but it will likely remain dependent on seaborne trade to access oil for at least the next decade, and it derives much of its wealth from producing goods for export.[124] Even if China successfully expands its capacity to import oil over land routes and shifts its economic model away from such strong dependence on exports, a blockade will likely retain the potential to impose considerable damage to the Chinese economy.

Finally, the United States could impose a blockade without having to maintain a large, permanent forward presence in the region during peacetime.[125] Having to deploy naval forces once a conflict has started would take time, but some restrainers view this as a feature rather than a bug because it would force allies to take their own defense more seriously and would build in more time to de-escalate before the United States became heavily involved.

Prevent a Successful Chinese Blockade or Coercive Missile Bombardment of Japan

Many advocates of restraint want Japan to remain an independent power that is capable of helping counterbalance China's influence in the region. Although they would prefer that Japan provide for its own defense without U.S. assistance, they recognize that Japan might need some support given China's greater size and growing power. A Chinese ground invasion of the Japanese home islands does not appear plausible within the next decade given the location of these islands and the significant number of forces that the PLA would need to commit to invade and occupy territory there. However, China has built a vast arsenal of missiles and an increasingly modern air force with which it could bombard key Japanese military and civil targets, and it has a considerable ability to interfere with the maritime trade upon which Japan is heavily dependent, which could be used in an effort to coerce Japan into complying with Chinese political demands. China also has significant cyber capabilities that it could use against military and civilian targets.

Prevent China from Seizing Control of the Ryukyu Islands

Beyond a general interest in upholding Japan's independence, some restrainers are attentive to specific aspects of Japan's geography. To limit China's ability to project maritime power, some advocates of restraint prefer to box China in geographically by keeping key geographic features that Chinese ships and aircraft would have to pass to enter the open ocean in the hands of independent states. Advocates of restraint are not willing to fight in all such cases.

---

[123] Posen, 2014, p. 94.

[124] Jeffrey Becker, *Securing China's Lifelines Across the Indian Ocean*, Newport, R.I.: China Maritime Studies Institute, U.S. Naval War College, China Maritime Report No. 11, December 2020; Wallace C. Gregson, Jr., and Jeffrey W. Hornung, "The United States Considers Reinforcing Its 'Pacific Sanctuary,'" *War on the Rocks*, April 12, 2021; Jennifer Lind and Daryl G. Press, "Markets or Mercantilism? How China Secures Its Energy Supplies," *International Security*, Vol. 42, No. 4, Spring 2018; Office of the Secretary of Defense, 2020, pp. 123, 133–134.

[125] Posen, 2014.

Most notably, Chinese control of Taiwan would facilitate China's ability to project power, but many advocates of restraint believe that the costs of trying to defend the island are prohibitively high. Still, there are other features that they might be willing to defend in at least some circumstances. The most salient feature that would be useful to keep in Japanese hands is the Ryukyu archipelago, which extends more than 1,000 km southwest from the Japanese island of Kyushu, to near the east coast of Taiwan. This island chain includes Okinawa, where the United States has a long-standing military presence.[126] For some advocates of restraint, the fact that these islands are part of Japan is sufficient to justify a U.S. response.[127]

The defense of the Ryukyu Islands would become significantly more difficult if China were to gain control of Taiwan. Advocates of restraint generally do not support the United States defending Taiwan from Chinese conquest. This does not mean that Taiwan would inevitably fall or would do so rapidly, but this outcome would become more likely without U.S. support. As a result, the likelihood and viability of an attack on Japan's southern Ryukyu Islands might also increase if the United States adopted a grand strategy of restraint. If China did gain control of Taiwan, control of the southern Ryukyus could become a new Chinese objective both for the security of Chinese-controlled Taiwan and for China's access to the Pacific. Moreover, the PLA would likely move capabilities, such as air defense and ASCM batteries, to Taiwan after gaining control. These systems would obstruct Japan's ability to move forces to the area to defend the southern Ryukyus from attack, whereas Chinese forces could quickly move across the relatively short distance from Taiwan to the nearby Japanese islands. Restrainers' concerns about striking mainland China would likely extend to Taiwan once it was under Chinese control, since China sees the island as part of its territory. If this meant that the PLA could operate from Taiwan without fear of attack, defending the southern Ryukyus would become extraordinarily difficult.

Prevent China from Crippling Japan's Air and Sea Power

To ensure that Japan remains an effective counterweight against China, advocates of restraint might wish to retain the capability to intervene if Japan appears to be at risk of a major military loss that would leave the Japan Self-Defense Forces (JSDF) severely weakened. Given the region's geography, the United States would be particularly concerned about a major degradation of Japan's air and sea power. This mission would not involve defending Japan in all cases or necessarily fighting in the lead. Instead, the United States would retain the capability to intervene in the case of a major war that threatened severe losses to Japan's military capabilities.

---

[126] Posen, 2014, p. 99. For a description of the Ryukyus, see "Ryukyu Islands," Encyclopaedia Britannica, last updated February 28, 2017.

[127] Emma Ashford, interview with the authors, video call, August 25, 2021.

Three Candidate Asia-Pacific Planning Scenarios for a Grand Strategy of Restraint

Contemporary analyses of U.S. force requirements in the Asia-Pacific typically center on scenarios involving defending Taiwan or fighting for control of the South or East China seas.[128] These are the contingencies that generally top restrainers' lists of potential wars in the region that the United States should avoid fighting. We have, therefore, selected three other scenarios that are representative of the kinds of conflicts that restrainers might view as worthy of preparing for to deter Chinese expansionism:

- China attacks Japan's armed forces and economy.
- After occupying Taiwan, China seizes the southern Ryukyu Islands.
- The United States imposes a distant blockade on China during a war between China and Japan.

We present these as stand-alone scenarios in the following three chapters, but they could conceivably all occur as part of a larger conflict between the United States and China, which would place correspondingly greater demands on U.S. military resources.

Although defending the U.S. homeland from an attack emanating from Asia would remain a priority under a grand strategy of restraint, we do not analyze a U.S. homeland defense scenario in detail, since it is already a U.S. priority and restraint advocates generally do not recommend approaches for it that are distinctively different from the status quo.

Like most planning scenarios, these are contingencies that are plausible rather than probable. China and the United States have powerful reasons not to go to war with each other (although the same has often been true of great powers in the past when deterrence failed). We include them on the list of scenarios not because they are likely to occur but because they are representative of conflicts that the United States might task the military to prepare for under a grand strategy of restraint.

---

[128] For examples of analyses considering such scenarios, see Eric Heginbotham, Michael Nixon, Forrest E. Morgan, Jacob L. Heim, Jeff Hagen, Sheng Li, Jeffrey Engstrom, Martin C. Libicki, Paul DeLuca, David A. Shlapak, David R. Frelinger, Burgess Laird, Kyle Brady, and Lyle J. Morris, *The U.S.-China Military Scorecard: Forces, Geography, and the Evolving Balance of Power, 1996–2017*, Santa Monica, Calif.: RAND Corporation, RR-392-AF, 2015; and David Ochmanek, Peter A. Wilson, Brenna Allen, John Speed Meyers, and Carter C. Price, *U.S. Military Capabilities and Forces for a Dangerous World: Rethinking the U.S. Approach to Force Planning*, Santa Monica, Calif.: RAND Corporation, RR-1782-1-RC, 2017. For a Taiwan scenario reportedly being a planning scenario as recently as DoD's 2010 Quadrennial Defense Review, see Larson, 2019, p. 238.

CHAPTER THREE

China Attacks Japan's Armed Forces and Economy

Because many restrainers are willing to use U.S. military power to preserve Japan as a major power that can balance against China (Chapter Two), this scenario focuses on threats to the Japanese armed forces and economy. In particular, the scenario considers Chinese air, cyber, and missile attacks against Japan's armed forces, infrastructure, and economic targets. China's objectives in this scenario are to coerce Japan into making concessions over a territorial dispute and to cripple Japan's air and naval power and its missile defenses. The territorial dispute is not a vital U.S. interest for restrainers, but restrainers would care about severe losses to the JSDF that would undermine Japan's ability act as a regional counterweight to China.[1] This chapter outlines what such a campaign might look like and its implications for U.S. military posture.

Our preliminary analysis of this scenario suggests that early intervention with U.S. air and naval forces would likely be necessary to preserve the JSDF as an effective force-in-being. Given qualitative and quantitative trends in the Sino-Japanese military balance that favor the PLA, China could hollow out large portions of Japan's air and maritime forces in the weeks that the United States would need to mobilize and deploy naval forces from the continental United States to Japan. U.S. airpower could deploy more quickly, but its responsiveness would depend on whether the United States and Japan had made previous preparations for basing and logistics support to sustain operations once the aircraft arrived. Japan's investments in its own military capabilities could change the U.S. capacity required, and efforts to make its defenses more resilient, including hardening infrastructure and augmenting ground-based missile defense, are particularly important. More in-depth analysis should explore how much support Japan would need and the capabilities and capacity that the United States should keep deployed forward in peacetime. Our preliminary analysis does suggest, however, that the United States would struggle to achieve its objectives in this type of scenario if it did not have some naval presence in the region during peacetime.

---

[1]   Other analysts outside the restraint camp have also suggested this type of scenario. See, for example, Ochmanek et al., 2017, p. 19.

Scenario Context and Assumptions

For this scenario, we assume that a restraint-oriented United States would retain security ties with Japan but seek to incentivize it to increase JSDF capabilities and reduce its reliance on the U.S. military, including by renegotiating the terms of the alliance and reducing the size of the U.S. military presence stationed in the country.[2] We assume that Japan would increase investments in its own defense as a result but that strengthening its armed forces would be a slow process and would face obstacles, such as domestic political opposition and recruitment challenges due to Japan's aging population.[3] Given strong, deep-seated anti-nuclear sentiment in Japan, we assume that Japan would not pursue nuclear weapons as long as the United States retains some commitment to its defense.[4] Our goal in this chapter is to imagine a conflict between China and Japan that would take place in this context and that would expand enough to draw in a restraint-oriented United States.

The scenario begins with an escalating confrontation that has grown out of the Sino-Japanese territorial dispute over the Senkaku/Diaoyu Islands and the maritime area surrounding them in the East China Sea.[5] In it, China demands that Japan acknowledge China's sovereignty over the islands and seeks to control the strategic space by declaring air and maritime exclusion zones around the Senkakus/Diaoyus that would prevent Japan from exercising administrative control and from accessing the waters and airspace around the islands.

---

[2]   Posen, 2014, p. 100. Although advocates of restraint do not explicitly say as much, this might involve changes to the defense cooperation guidelines that manage security relations between the two countries (Ministry of Foreign Affairs of Japan, *The Guidelines for Japan-U.S. Defense Cooperation*, Tokyo, April 27, 2015).

[3]   Recent calls from Japan's ruling Liberal Democratic Party to double defense spending are one potential indication that rising concerns about China might increase Japan's willingness to invest more in its armed forces, but to what extent remains to be seen (Tim Kelly and Ju-min Park, "Analysis: With an Eye on China, Japan's Ruling Party Makes Unprecedented Defence Spending Pledge," Reuters, October 13, 2021). On the defense implications of Japan's demographics, see Yoshimitsu Sato, "Can the Japan Self-Defense Force Age Gracefully?" *The Diplomat*, September 18, 2019. On anti-militarism and Japan's security policies, see Yasuhiro Izumikawa, "Explaining Japanese Antimilitarism: Normative and Realist Constraints on Japan's Security Policy," *International Security*, Vol. 35, No. 2, Fall 2010.

[4]   Llewelyn Hughes, "Why Japan Will Not Go Nuclear (Yet): International and Domestic Constraints on the Nuclearization of Japan," *International Security*, Vol. 31, No. 4, Spring 2007.

[5]   For views that this is the most likely scenario for the U.S. defense of Japan, see Michael Beckley, "The Emerging Military Balance in East Asia: How China's Neighbors Can Check Chinese Naval Expansion," *International Security*, Vol. 42, No. 2, 2017, p. 95; Timothy R. Heath, "Chinese Political and Military Thinking Regarding Taiwan and the East and South China Seas," testimony presented before the U.S.-China Economic and Security Review Commission on April 13, 2017, Santa Monica, Calif.: RAND Corporation, CT-470, 2017; Eric Heginbotham and Richard J. Samuels, "Active Denial: Redesigning Japan's Response to China's Military Challenge," *International Security*, Vol. 42, No. 4, Spring 2018; and Michael E. O'Hanlon, *The Senkaku Paradox: Risking Great Power War over Small Stakes*, Washington, D.C.: Brookings Institution Press, 2019, p. 2.

The PLA deploys surface ships, submarines, and air assets into the East China Sea to enforce the exclusion zones.[6]

While U.S. restrainers would not fight to defend this disputed territory as an end in itself given its relatively minor significance to the balance of power in Asia, Japan would likely respond regardless of U.S. preferences because it considers the Senkakus/Diaoyus to be Japanese territory.[7] Tokyo may also worry that failing to challenge China's military actions would invite further Chinese aggression.[8] Therefore, in the scenario, Japanese air and naval forces deploy to contest the exclusion zones. A series of engagements over several days escalates from warning shots to attacks, and the result is that both sides lose ships and aircraft and there are substantial casualties. The PLAN suffers unexpectedly heavy losses from JMSDF submarine attacks, but, given the PLA's greater naval and missile capabilities, Japanese surface forces withdraw to safer locations.

Despite China's stronger military position, Japan refuses to accede to China's political demands. Given public support for the conflict, the partial Japanese retreat, and calls to avenge casualties, Beijing privately decides to use the opportunity to dramatically reduce Japan's ability to project military power beyond its shores, including to challenge China's de facto control of the East China Sea.[9] Publicly, China threatens to attack Japan's power-projection capabilities that could contest China's control unless Japan formally accepts the loss of the Senkakus/Diaoyus. When Japan does not comply, China follows through on the threat.

PLA Attacks on Japan

China would likely begin its campaign to attack Japan's power-projection capabilities with air, cyber, and missile attacks against Japanese air and missile defenses, JASDF bases, JMSDF ships and facilities, and related military and dual-use targets, including critical infrastruc-

---

[6] This would be consistent with China's current gray zone strategy in the East China Sea to exert maritime control through its naval and increasingly militarized coast guard forces. For a discussion of China's use of these capabilities around the Senkaku/Diaoyu Islands in the past, see Alessio Patalano, "When Strategy Is 'Hybrid' and Not 'Grey': Reviewing Chinese Military and Constabulary Coercion at Sea," *Pacific Review*, Vol. 31, No. 6, 2018.

[7] On Japan's commitment to its legal claims over the islands and willingness to defend them, see Japan Ministry of Foreign Affairs, "Senkaku Islands Q&A," webpage, April 13, 2016; and Brad Lendon and Blake Essig, "Japan's Defense Minister Draws Red Line in Island Dispute with China," CNN, September 16, 2021.

[8] For a discussion of this general logic, see Todd S. Sechser, "Goliath's Curse: Coercive Threats and Asymmetric Power," *International Organization*, Vol. 64, No. 4, Fall 2010.

[9] China's strategy in this scenario resembles that of the United States in early 1991, when it sought to compel Iraqi forces to leave Kuwait but also to cripple Iraq's army by, in the words of General Colin Powell, leaving "smoking tanks as kilometer fence posts all the way to Baghdad" (Robert A. Pape, *Bombing to Win: Air Power and Coercion in War*, Ithaca, N.Y.: Cornell University Press, 1996, p. 224). This is not necessarily a likely Chinese response in a Senkakus/Diaoyus scenario, but restrainers concerned with the defensive viability of Japan might want to have the capability to respond to an expansion of Chinese war aims of this kind.

ture, anti-ship missile batteries, command and control (C2) facilities, and radar installations.[10] Should Japan refuse to comply with China's demands, China could expand its attacks to Japanese ports and inbound shipping.[11] Attacks on maritime commerce would ostensibly serve the goal of limiting Japanese imports of military supplies, but their principal purpose would be to encourage Tokyo to submit to Chinese demands by demonstrating to the Japanese government and populace that China can punish them at will if they fail to cooperate.

The PLA has considerable military capabilities to execute such a campaign, including a large inventory of ballistic missiles and LACMs (Table 3.1). In 2021, DoD estimated that China had 600 MRBMs and hundreds of ground- and air-launched cruise missiles that could reach the Japanese home islands (Figure 3.1).[12] These missiles, some of which can carry advanced warheads, including submunitions for attacking area targets, could strike fixed targets, including aircraft parking areas and air base facilities, berthed ships, and port facilities.[13] Ballistic missiles would be especially useful for destroying Japan's air defense radars and missile batteries. The PLAAF would likely initially rely heavily on air-launched cruise missiles from bombers to supplement ground-launched missile attacks, and it would later launch penetrating air attacks if it succeeded in substantially degrading Japanese air

TABLE 3.1

Chinese Surface-to-Surface Missile Inventories, 2021

System	Launchers	Missiles	Estimated Range
ICBM	100	150	> 5,500 km
IRBM	200	300	3,000–5,500 km
MRBM	250	600	1,000–3,000 km
SRBM	250	1,000	300–1,000 km
GLCM	100	300	> 1,500 km

SOURCE: Office of the Secretary of Defense, 2021, p. 163.
NOTES: GLCM = ground-launched cruise missile; SRBM = short-range ballistic missile. Air- and sea-launched cruise missiles and ASCMs are not shown.

---

[10] This assessment is based in part on analysis of China's military doctrine in a campaign against Taiwan (Beckley, 2017, p. 84; Ian Easton, *The Chinese Invasion Threat: Taiwan's Defense and American Strategy in Asia*, Arlington, Va.: Project 2049 Institute, 2017; Heginbotham et al., 2015, pp. 98–100; Office of the Secretary of Defense, 2020, p. 113). China would likely employ other tools as well, such as economic coercion, but we focus here on military means, which would most directly inform U.S. military requirements.

[11] The PLA could launch an initial campaign of missile attacks and then pause for potential negotiations. Chinese military campaign planning for a Taiwan contingency highlights this tactic in a "joint firepower strike operation," which starts with intermittent missile and air strikes against key targets in Taiwan to leave room for political negotiations (Ian Easton, *China's Top Five War Plans*, Arlington, Va.: Project 2049 Institute, Policy Brief 19-001, 2019).

[12] Office of the Secretary of Defense, 2021, p. 163.

[13] Office of the Secretary of Defense, 2020, p. 81.

FIGURE 3.1

Chinese Missile Ranges

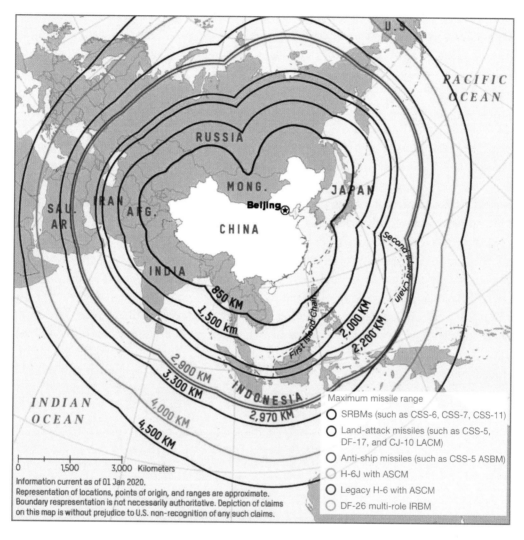

SOURCE: Office of the Secretary of Defense, 2020, p. 57.

defenses.[14] After initial missile strikes on Japan's air defense systems, Chinese fighters would likely begin to target Japanese aircraft in air-to-air engagements. The PLARF could use its medium- and intermediate-range ASBMs to attack major enemy surface ships at sea in concert with air- and sea-launched ASCMs. China could also use ASCMs to target Japan-bound

---

[14] Heginbotham and Samuels, 2018, pp. 149–150.

merchant ships. This campaign would likely include conducting cyberattacks against JSDF military installations and systems and jamming Japan's military communications.[15]

If U.S. forces are present in Japan prior to the Chinese attack, China could intentionally target them along with Japanese forces. It is possible that Beijing might defer strikes as long as the United States did not participate in the fighting around the Senkakus/Diaoyus, but once U.S. forces actively participate in defending Japan, the PLA would presumably attack them in turn.[16]

The PLA might also expand its missile campaign to target Japanese port infrastructure, including high-speed cranes and docks and liquified natural gas and oil terminals, to further cripple Japan's ability to sustain military operations and to threaten the Japanese economy.[17] The PLA could mine the entrance of key Japanese harbors to dissuade ships from entering, patrol harbor approaches with submarines to threaten JMSDF forces, and use fighters to attack JASDF fighters and MPA attempting to protect ports and escort shipping.[18] China's cyber capabilities would also offer nonkinetic options for further disrupting Japan's economy by attacking transportation, energy, and financial infrastructure.[19]

Such a campaign would have significant effects on Japan's maritime trade and economy. Chinese attacks on ports and shipping would not completely cut off Japan's access to trade, especially because Japan could rely on well-developed ports on its east coast, but Japan's reliance on food and energy imports makes it particularly susceptible to disruptions.[20] Its economy also relies heavily on trade with China, which accounts for 18 percent of its exports and 23 percent of its imports, and which Beijing could cut off at will.[21] Furthermore, Japan depends on seaborne trade for crude oil, which it imports at a rate of approximately 2,900,000

---

[15] Fiona S. Cunningham, "Testimony Before the U.S.-China Economic and Security Review Commission," hearing on "Deterring PRC Aggression Towards Taiwan," February 18, 2021, Washington, D.C.: U.S.-China Economic and Security Review Commission, 2021, p. 4; Oriana Skylar Mastro, "The Taiwan Temptation: Why Beijing Might Resort to Force," *Foreign Affairs*, Vol. 100, No. 4, July–August 2021.

[16] Some U.S. forces are colocated on bases with Japanese forces. If this arrangement were still in place, then Chinese strikes on Japanese forces might inadvertently harm U.S. forces or facilities.

[17] China would face additional international blowback for expanding the conflict against civilian infrastructure and shipping, so it might forgo this option.

[18] PLA writings about a blockade of Taiwan discuss mining. Publications describe a three-ring blockade consisting of mines outside commercial ports, patrols of surface ships and submarines, and a final ring up to 50 nm around Taiwan that naval aircraft would patrol. See Easton, 2017, pp. 101–102.

[19] Chinese writings suggest that China would employ information operations and cyber campaigns in a conflict. In this scenario, Chinese actions could include conducting cyberattacks against JSDF military installations and systems and jamming Japan's military communications. See Cunningham, 2021, p. 4; and Mastro, 2021.

[20] Biddle and Oelrich, 2016, p. 17. Japan depended on food imports for around 62 percent of its caloric consumption in 2019 ("Japan's Food Self-Sufficiency Rate Marks 38 Percent in Fiscal 2019, Far from Its Target of 45 Percent," *Japan Agricultural News*, August 11, 2020).

[21] Central Intelligence Agency, "Japan," *World Factbook*, June 9, 2021.

barrels per day (bpd) while producing only 3,570 bpd domestically.[22] Japan's strategic petro-leum reserve contains around 290 million barrels of crude oil, and private companies hold another 70 million barrels in reserves.[23] As a result, Chinese attacks on the trade on which Japan's population and military depend would cause significant disruptions in Japan.

Japanese and U.S. Approaches

Although this scenario begins with China and Japan fighting for control of part of the East China Sea, we assume that the fate of the Senkakus/Diaoyus would take second place in Tokyo's hierarchy of concerns. The more pressing issue would be Chinese attacks on Japan's military forces and economy. Japan's response would have several elements, including defend-ing against PLAN attacks on Japanese ports, commerce, and the JSDF; air and missile attacks on key military targets and ports; and cyberattacks on Japan's military and civilian targets.

Japan's current defense strategy and force posture are oriented around a shield-and-spear model in which Japan provides defensive capabilities (the shield) designed to last only until the United States intervenes. The United States then provides greater force capacity and long-range strike capabilities (the spear).[24] Because Japan's strategy relies on U.S. assistance for longer-range capabilities, its military preparations have emphasized defending its home islands through developing a robust destroyer and submarine fleet to protect littoral waters and conduct ASW and ISR missions, as well as air and missile defense capabilities to defend Japanese airspace.[25]

The PLAN has quantitative advantages over the JMSDF, and its shipboard ASCMs have longer ranges (as noted in Chapter Two). This means that JMSDF surface vessels would suffer rapid attrition if they sought to directly engage the PLAN in a large fleet-on-fleet engage-ment. As a result, given the scale of the threat, it is unlikely that Japan would concentrate its surface fleet in the disputed maritime area around the Senkakus/Diaoyus at the outbreak of a crisis. Japan's investment in additional ASCM capabilities in the Ryukyu Islands could assist

[22] Fotios Katsoulas, "Monthly Report: Japan's Crude Imports Soar to 2.9MMbpd in August," IHS Markit, August 18, 2021; Knoema, "Japan - Production of Crude Oil Including Lease Condensate," webpage, undated).

[23] "Biden Wants Major Oil Reserve Sales. That's Not Easy in Asia," Bloomberg, last updated November 19, 2021; Takeo Kumagai, "Japan to Sell Part of National Oil Reserves by Advancing Crude Grade Replacement Plans," S&P Global, November 24, 2021.

[24] Edmund Burke, Timothy R. Heath, Jeffrey W. Hornung, Logan Ma, Lyle J. Morris, and Michael S. Chase, *China's Military Activities in the East China Sea: Implications for Japan's Air Self-Defense Force*, Santa Monica, Calif.: RAND Corporation, RR-2574-AF, 2018, p. 4; Heginbotham and Samuels, 2018, pp. 135–137; Hornung, 2020a, pp. ix, 13.

[25] On long-term shifts in Japan's defense strategy, see Scott Harold, Koichiro Bansho, Jeffrey W. Hornung, Koichi Isobe, and Richard L. Simcock II, *U.S.-Japan Alliance Conference: Meeting the Challenge of Amphibi-ous Operations*, Santa Monica, Calif.: RAND Corporation, CF-387-GOJ, 2018, pp. 3–4. For Japan's charac-terization of its strategy for the "defense of Japan's remote islands," see Japan Ministry of Defense, *Defense of Japan 2020*, Tokyo, 2020a, p. 28; and Hornung, 2020a, pp. x–xi.

the JSDF in targeting Chinese forces around the Senkakus/Diaoyus, which could provide the JMSDF with some freedom of maneuver to counter the PLAN. But we expect that as soon as China expanded the conflict beyond the Senkakus/Diaoyus, any portion of the JMSDF surface fleet in that area would likely fall back toward the home islands to focus on escort missions for Japan's merchant fleet.

Especially in the early stages of the conflict, Japan's capable submarine force would play an important role in directly engaging the PLAN and conducting ASW. Japan has ground-based and air-launched anti-ship missiles in the home islands that it could employ if China uses surface ships closer to Japan's coast in its attacks on Japanese ports and shipping. Although Japan is already investing in ASCM capabilities in the Southwest Islands, as well as developing standoff missile capabilities, additional investment in longer-range ASCMs would be useful in a strategy to counter the PLAN.

Japan has some capability to defend its territory from a Chinese air and missile campaign. JMSDF Aegis air defense destroyers with Standard Missile-3 missiles and JASDF land-based Patriot Advanced Capability-3 missile batteries provide theater ballistic missile defense capabilities (as noted in Chapter Two). But these systems have limited engagement capacity and numbers of interceptor missiles, and the mobility of the Patriots is poor relative to ballistic missile flight times from China, which makes them vulnerable to saturation attacks from large salvos of Chinese missiles.[26] Japan is also improving its ability to defend against PLA aircraft and cruise missiles by upgrading its F-15 fighters and procuring more-advanced combat aircraft, including F-35Bs that are capable of operating at dispersed locations away from major bases, as well as away from Japan's light aircraft carriers.[27]

The JSDF operates from some 20 bases across 2,000 mi of territory, and this reduces its vulnerability to Chinese strikes to some extent.[28] Dispersing air and maritime forces more extensively would make the force less vulnerable, including by lowering the risk of losing large numbers of air and naval assets in a single strike, making it more complicated for Chinese forces to track and target Japanese forces, expanding the number of targets that China would need to strike over a larger geographic distance, and reducing Japan's reliance on the infrastructure of any given air or naval facility.[29] However, Japan currently lacks the supporting capabilities needed to use a larger number of operating locations for survivability. For example, lack of sealift and oilers would make it difficult for the JMSDF to move supplies and

---

[26] For a discussion of Japan's missile defense systems, see Hornung, 2020a, pp. 58–65. Japan has scuttled plans for more investment in these systems, but it might revisit these plans if it perceives that the threat from China is growing in the future (Jeffrey W. Hornung, "Japan Is Canceling a U.S. Missile Defense System," *Foreign Policy*, July 2, 2020b).

[27] Beckley, 2017.

[28] In addition to 20 air bases, Japan has 11 naval bases and 14 naval aviation bases (Beckley, 2017, p. 98).

[29] For a more detailed discussion of the survivability benefits of distributed operations, see Miranda Priebe, Alan J. Vick, Jacob L. Heim, and Meagan L. Smith, *Distributed Operations in a Contested Environment: Implications for USAF Force Presentation*, Santa Monica, Calif.: RAND Corporation, RR-2959-AF, 2019.

equipment to enable the use of civilian ports as additional locations for resupply and operational support during a conflict. Similarly, dispersed air basing requires larger numbers of maintenance and security personnel and additional ground support equipment, while insufficient airlift could inhibit the movement of supplies and equipment among a larger number of air bases. Pre-positioning supplies in advance of conflict or investing in more lift would help enable distributed operations that could improve the JSDF's survivability against air and missile attacks.[30]

As noted in Chapter Two, Japan has increased its investment in cyber defenses, but it remains vulnerable. To be prepared for a scenario like this one, Japan would need to focus in particular on bolstering defenses against Chinese cyberattacks targeting its military forces, import terminals, and other port operations.[31]

To summarize, given the PLA's numerical and qualitative advantages, the JSDF's ability to defend Japan against a Chinese missile campaign and attacks on Japanese ports and shipping is limited without U.S. support. In particular, the PLA's increased development and growing arsenal of precision strike missiles, along with longer-range ASCMs deployed on PLAN surface ships, enhance China's ability to erode the JSDF's air and missile defenses. Substantial reduction in JSDF capability would undermine Japan's ability to defend itself from China, to protect its economic interests, and to act as a counterweight to Beijing in the future.

Once a confrontation between China and Japan appeared likely to escalate, U.S. naval and air forces based in Japan would disperse for survivability—the naval forces out to sea and the air forces to additional bases in Japan or to locations farther away, such as Guam. Once the United States entered the conflict, U.S. Navy surface ships and submarines could attack PLAN forces that were targeting JSDF naval and air assets. For example, the U.S. Navy could bring a substantial number of surface ships to the outer range of Chinese ASBMs and then rely on standoff capabilities and submarines to sink PLAN ships and target military aircraft. U.S. military aircraft could also shoot down incoming Chinese cruise missiles and aircraft. To counter China's attacks on Japanese ports and shipping, the United States could use its forward-deployed ships and submarines to conduct ASW operations and to defend key Japanese ports from Chinese naval and air forces. Finally, the United States might opt to use non-kinetic counterspace capabilities to degrade Chinese communications and the ISR systems that support China's missile targeting capabilities.

Although the focus of this report is on U.S. military measures, the United States would also have a variety of other methods to aid Japan. For example, the United States is Japan's leading supplier of agricultural imports, with a 25-percent market share in 2017, and it could increase food exports to Japan if Chinese attacks on merchant shipping deterred other countries from exporting.[32] The United States could also supply significant amounts of crude oil

---

[30] Hornung, 2020a, pp. xiii, 54.

[31] Lewis, 2015, pp. 10–11.

[32] Kimberly Marie, *United States Agricultural Exports to Japan Remain Promising*, Washington, D.C.: U.S. Department of Agriculture, International Agricultural Trade Report, June 5, 2018.

to Japan. It currently exports around 400,000 bpd to China, and it could divert those shipments to Japan during a conflict.[33] These efforts would operate in tandem with the military campaign, such as by using U.S. Navy surface ships for convoys of oil tankers.

Implications for U.S. Posture and Force Structure

The United States currently has an extensive military posture in the Indo-Pacific. The forces that are currently assigned to U.S. Indo-Pacific Command's area of responsibility include around 200 ships, 1,100 aircraft, and 130,000 personnel in the U.S. Pacific Fleet; two Marine Expeditionary Forces comprising 86,000 marines; around 400 aircraft and 46,000 personnel in the U.S. Pacific Air Forces; and 106,000 U.S. Army personnel with 300 aircraft.[34] Additional forces in Alaska, Washington, and California are earmarked to support U.S. Indo-Pacific Command's mission but technically fall within U.S. Northern Command's area of responsibility.[35] Many of U.S. Indo-Pacific Command's forces operate in or from the United States and U.S. territories, including Hawaii, two major air and naval bases in Guam, and pre-positioned U.S. Navy logistics ships at Guam and the nearby island of Saipan in the Northern Marianas. In Japan, the United States permanently stations 55,000 military personnel, which is its largest forward deployment in the world, and it has access to around 100 military facilities, including major air bases at Misawa, Yokota, and Kadena and naval bases at Yokosuka,

---

[33] Oceana Zhou, "China's 2020 Crude Imports from US Surge 211% to 396,000 b/d, Valued at $6.28 Bil," S&P Global Platts, January 20, 2021.

[34] U.S. Indo-Pacific Command, "About USINDOPACOM," webpage, undated a.

[35] Dakota L. Wood, ed., *2021 Index of U.S. Military Strength*, Washington, D.C.: Heritage Foundation, 2021, p. 197. The Pacific Fleet is headquartered at Pearl Harbor, and the Pacific Air Fleet (PACAF) is headquartered at Hickam Air Force Base. According to the U.S. Navy, there are "25 surface ships and submarines homeported at Pearl Harbor, as well as up to 25 operational aircraft at Marine Corps Base Hawaii, Kaneohe" (Commander, Navy Region Hawaii, "Fleet Information," webpage, undated). PACAF stations fighters, bombers, and airlift capabilities in Hawaii, and there are also Army and Marine Corps deployments (David J. Berteau, Michael J. Green, Gregory T. Kiley, Nicholas F. Szechenyi, Ernest Z. Bower, Victor Cha, Karl F. Inderfurth, Christopher K. Johnson, Gary A. Powell, and Stephanie Sanok, *U.S. Force Posture Strategy in the Asia Pacific Region: An Independent Assessment*, Washington, D.C.: Center for Strategic and International Studies, 2012, p. 56). U.S. Naval Base Guam is the homeport for three nuclear-powered attack submarines, and Andersen Air Force Base hosts rotational deployments of bombers, an unmanned ISR squadron, and tankers (Wood, 2021, p. 197; Szechenyi et al., 2012, p. 54). On U.S. presence in the Northern Marianas, see Szechenyi et al., 2012, pp. 57–60; and Wood, 2021, p. 197.

Atsugi, and Sasebo.[36] The United States also has a large presence in South Korea and a smaller presence in several other countries in the Indo-Pacific region.[37]

To defend Japan and ensure that a substantial portion of Japan's forces survive the conflict in this scenario, the United States would want to sustain some elements of this posture. However, there are other elements of current U.S. posture in the region that would no longer be necessary under a grand strategy of restraint.

China's military advantages over Japan are significant enough that the United States would likely need to mobilize naval forces quickly in this scenario to forestall the destruction of much of the JMSDF. Given the quantitative advantages of the PLAN, even a drastic increase in Japan's shipbuilding is likely to prove insufficient to enable the JMSDF to compete in fleet-on-fleet engagements on a large scale with China's navy in the next decade. The PLAN's emphasis on equipping its surface ships with ASCMs that outrange the JSDF's missile arsenal makes the JMSDF even more vulnerable. This has two implications in the next decade. First, the JMSDF surface fleet could experience relatively quick attrition if it directly engaged with Chinese forces. The JMSDF could rely primarily on its small but capable submarine fleet for ASW and limit its surface fleet's direct engagements with the Chinese forces in order to prioritize its survival. This would leave Japan's coasts and commercial vessels more vulnerable to the PLAN, although Japan's investments in longer-range ASCMs would decrease this vulnerability. Second, regardless of how long the JMSDF could hold out, China's quantitatively superior naval forces could continue to attack military targets along the Japanese coast, as well as commerce and ports.[38]

At least some U.S. naval forces would likely need to be in the region at the outset of the conflict to mobilize quickly enough to slow the JSDF's attrition. There is little public analysis on the timelines necessary for U.S. force deployment to a regional conflict. However, we estimate that it would take at least two weeks for surface vessels to transit from the U.S. West

---

[36] Emma Chanlett-Avery, Caitlin Campbell, and Joshua A. Williams, *The U.S.-Japan Alliance*, Washington, D.C.: Congressional Research Service, RL33740, June 13, 2019, p. 1; U.S. Government Accountability Office, *Burden Sharing: Benefits and Costs Associated with the U.S. Military Presence in Japan and South Korea*, Washington, D.C., 2021.

[37] The U.S. military presence in South Korea includes about 31,000 military personnel (International Institute for Strategic Studies, 2021a, p. 280). Other deployments include approximately 700 military personnel and radar and signals intelligence infrastructure in Australia, in addition to an annual rotational deployment of marines; several hundred forces involved in counterterrorism operations in the Philippines; 200 military personnel at a naval support facility in Singapore that hosts rotational deployments of littoral combat ships; and 300 personnel in Thailand (International Institute for Strategic Studies, 2021a, pp. 243, 296, 299, 307; Marine Rotational Force, "U.S. Marines Complete Their Ninth Rotation in Australia," U.S. Indo-Pacific Command, October 22, 2020).

[38] Toshi Yoshihara, *Dragon Against the Sun: Chinese Views of Japanese Seapower*, Washington, D.C.: Center for Strategic and Budgetary Assessments, 2020a, pp. 7–22.

Coast to Guam.[39] Even transiting from Hawaii might take around ten days.[40] In addition to transit time, the total time for deployment to the conflict zone would depend on how combat ready these forces were at the outset of a conflict and, therefore, how quickly they could leave the United States.[41] The key question, therefore, is whether Japan could hold out on its own for two weeks or more while the U.S. Navy deployed. Modeling a China-Japan naval confrontation is outside the scope of this analysis. This means that there is uncertainty about how Japan would fare on its own in this time frame. Considering China's quantitative and qualitative advantages, we anticipate that Japan could plausibly suffer serious losses, potentially leaving it open to Chinese coercion in the meantime and significantly reducing its military power. In the absence of more-detailed analysis of these questions, a risk-averse restrainer concerned with the defense of Japan would therefore likely err on the side of caution and maintain some U.S. naval forces in theater. However, restrainers and other military analysts should continue to examine Japanese self-defense capabilities and U.S. naval deployment timelines in more detail to validate this preliminary assessment.

Regardless of where U.S. naval forces are based in peacetime, locations outside Japan might be preferable once a conflict has begun. First, China has several ways to attack ports, air bases, and other facilities throughout the region, including missiles and unmanned aerial

---

[39] To make this calculation, we assumed that U.S. surface vessels would deploy at a speed similar to their speed in the past in wartime. To estimate this speed, we used approximate timelines and distances from Operation Enduring Freedom (2001), when the United States was rapidly deploying forces to fight the Taliban in Afghanistan. We were unable to identify any more-recent deployments under similar time pressures. In 2001, the USS *Theodore Roosevelt* deployed from Norfolk, Virginia, on September 19, arriving in the Northern Arabian Sea on October 15. For an approximate distance, we assumed that the ship traveled from Norfolk to the port of Karachi, Pakistan, transiting by way of the Strait of Gibraltar and the Suez Canal. For our hypothetical China-Japan conflict scenario, we assumed that U.S. vessels would transit from San Diego, California, to Guam at a similar speed (13 knots). This resulted in an estimated 17 days. This analogy is imperfect because the route is different. For example, it is possible that a more direct route on the ocean could be faster than transit through international straits. Unfortunately, we do not have a recent wartime deployment through the Pacific to use as a comparison. For a peacetime deployment of the same carrier from San Diego to Guam (by way of Hawaii), we found a somewhat slower speed than what we calculated above. The total transit time was approximately 21 days. See U.S. Naval Institute Staff, "USNI News Fleet and Marine Tracker: Jan 20, 2020," USNI News, last updated February 10, 2020. Together, these examples suggest something on the order of at least weeks for deployment from the continental United States when accounting for transit times and preparations to deploy. For distances between key ports, see National Geospatial-Intelligence Agency, *Pub. 151: Distances Between Ports*, 11th ed., Bethesda, Md., 2001. For information on the USS *Theodore Roosevelt*'s timeline, see Gregory Bereiter, *The U.S. Navy in Operation Enduring Freedom, 2001–2002*, Washington, D.C.: Naval History and Heritage Command, 2016. Sadler calculates a similar transit time from San Diego to Guam by assuming that U.S. naval vessels travel at 15 knots (Brent Sadler, "U.S. Navy," in Dakota L. Wood, ed., *2022 Index of U.S. Military Strength*, Washington, D.C.: Heritage Foundation, 2022, p. 390).

[40] Using the calculation in the previous footnote, we assumed sailing at 13 knots from Pearl Harbor in Hawaii to Apra in Guam.

[41] The U.S. Navy has had recurring issues with meeting deployment timelines for surface ship readiness (David B. Larter, "Surface Ship Readiness Continues to Struggle, US Navy Inspections Show," *Defense News*, March 3, 2021).

vehicles (UAVs). The closer that the facilities are to China, the greater the threat they face from PLA missile forces.[42] The JMSDF would face challenges dispersing and supplying its own forces from a small number of naval bases while under attack, given limited sealift capacity that would make the movement of equipment and supplies to civilian ports and underway replenishment more difficult, particularly in a conflict. To reduce demand on these facilities, the United States might want to disperse its forces farther out to sea at the beginning of the conflict and use locations farther away for resupply and repair. Other options for forward-deployed naval forces include Guam and Australia, where the government is considering granting the U.S. Navy greater access.[43] The U.S. Navy would also want to maintain enough sealift capacity (oilers, repair vessels, logistics ships) for underway replenishment, which would reduce its reliance on a small number of ports.[44]

U.S. land-based air forces, including MPA and fighters, would be central to a scenario like this one. As with naval forces, we are unaware of any unclassified analysis of how well Japan could defend its airspace on its own without U.S. support. Japan has a capable air force that can be expected to fare well against the PLAAF in individual engagements. The real challenge for Japan is capacity—the number of aircraft it could bring to bear against China's larger air force, particularly while being attacked at its bases by Chinese missiles. A basic examination of China's and Japan's relative military capabilities leads us to assess that the considerably smaller JASDF would likely struggle over a prolonged period to defend Japan's airspace against a large-scale attack by China given the size of China's air force, its large cruise missile arsenal, and its current and future investments in unmanned aircraft.[45] Therefore, U.S. airpower would likely be needed to defend Japanese airspace effectively, as well as to locate and target PLAN maritime forces. Carrier-based aircraft could contribute significantly; however, U.S. aircraft carriers have limited capacity—a U.S. carrier's air wing normally includes fewer than 50 fighters for both fleet defense and more offensive operations—and would need

---

[42] Alan J. Vick, Sean M. Zeigler, Julia Brackup, and John Speed Meyers, *Air Base Defense: Rethinking Army and Air Force Roles and Functions*, Santa Monica, Calif.: RAND Corporation, RR-4368-AF, 2020.

[43] Daniel Hurst, "Peter Dutton Flags More US Troops on Australian Soil Citing Potential China Conflict," *The Guardian*, June 10, 2021; Commander, Navy Installations Command, "Commander, Joint Region Marianas: Naval Base Guam," webpage, undated. The United States could, in theory, consider other locations, such as the Philippines and Singapore, but, as noted above, these options seem less likely under a grand strategy of restraint.

[44] Recent analysis on the challenges that U.S. sealift would face in conflict include not enough ships and an aging fleet that the U.S. Navy cannot easily replace. Even if the United States reduced the size of the Navy under a grand strategy of restraint, it would still need to invest in maintaining and potentially upgrading U.S. sealift, particularly if U.S. naval forces are arriving in the region from greater distances and would require more at-sea replenishment to sustain operations (Bryan Clark, Timothy A. Walton, and Adam Lemon, *Strengthening the U.S. Defense Maritime Industrial Base: A Plan to Improve Maritime Industry's Contribution to National Security*, Washington, D.C.: Center for Strategic and Budgetary Assessment, 2020; Elee Wakim, "Sealift Is America's Achilles Heel in the Age of Great Power Competition," *War on the Rocks*, January 18, 2019).

[45] For a description of the challenges that the JASDF has, see Hornung, 2020a, pp. 40–43.

to consider the risks of operating within the range of Chinese anti-ship missiles. Minimizing this risk by operating U.S. carrier strike groups farther from China would require naval aircraft to spend more time transiting to Japan, and, therefore, they could not spend as much time defending its airspace, and tanker requirements would also increase. To generate an amount of U.S. defensive counterair (DCA) protection over Japan that is comparable to the prewar size of the JASDF's fighter force structure (more than 300 aircraft), for example, land-based airpower either already in the region or deployed from the United States would be essential.[46]

In contrast to U.S. naval assets, there is less-compelling evidence that the United States would need to station land-based airpower in Asia during peacetime for these forces to contribute effectively during a conflict. In the past, when U.S. Air Force aircraft in the continental United States have been at a high level of readiness and have had well-prepared bases to fall in on, aircraft have arrived in theater and carried out operations within days.[47] Deploying this quickly in the event of conflict would require maintaining those air forces at a high level of readiness and making substantial peacetime preparations, including ongoing maintenance at air bases in the region. Continued exercises on combined operations with Japanese forces would also be important to ensure that the forces could quickly and effectively operate together in wartime.[48] Without more-detailed analysis of Japan's ability to defend its airspace against a large-scale Chinese air and missile attack and U.S. deployment timelines, it is difficult to know whether deploying forces could arrive quickly enough to meet U.S. objectives. Therefore, additional analysis is necessary to confirm this preliminary assessment.

In the face of uncertainty about how well Japan can defend its own airspace, and anticipating that U.S. forces would be needed in the event of conflict, some restrainers might wish to err on the side of caution and retain a permanent U.S. Air Force presence in Japan. Other restrainers might worry more about the presence of U.S. airpower discouraging burden-sharing and would therefore be more willing to take the risks associated with not having U.S. aircraft based in Japan during peacetime.

---

[46] Assuming that the JASDF would begin a conflict against China with its hands full trying to provide DCA against air and cruise missile attacks and would suffer substantial losses from PLA strikes on its bases, this represents a reasonable benchmark to consider, but the number of fighter sorties actually required in such a scenario would depend on many factors, and, as with carrier-based airpower, the number of aircraft needed to generate them would be greatly affected by the choice of basing locations. Flying combat air patrols from Guam, which is more than 2,500 km from most of Japan, would be equivalent to doing the same over Washington with fighters based in Denver.

[47] Establishing and deploying forces to bases often took longer during the wars in Iraq and Afghanistan because of the time it took to gain access from nearby countries and to develop the required infrastructure. In the case of a Chinese attack on Japan, we assume that Japan would quickly grant permission to U.S. forces to access its bases and would, in peacetime, be willing to maintain facilities to enable the rapid deployment of U.S. forces in the event of war (Robert S. Tripp, Kristin F. Lynch, John G. Drew, and Edward W. Chan, *Supporting Air and Space Expeditionary Forces: Lessons from Operation Enduring Freedom*, Santa Monica, Calif.: RAND Corporation, MR-1819-AF, 2004, pp. 43–48).

[48] For a current example of such exercises, see Pacific Air Forces, "US, Japan, Australia Converge on Guam for Cope North 21," February 2, 2021.

Beyond deciding where to base air forces in peacetime, restrainers would need to consider where to base air forces in the event of war. The United States would face trade-offs in deciding where to base its aircraft, particularly fighters, during the conflict. Aircraft operating from Japan would be at greater risk from Chinese missiles, while aircraft operating from Guam, the Northern Marianas, or other places in the Pacific would be under somewhat less threat but would have to fly farther to operate against Chinese forces. As a result, the United States would need more aircraft and crews to generate a similar level of combat power from these more distant locations.[49] Bombers and other large aircraft that have longer ranges but are too large for most hardened aircraft shelters would operate from more-distant locations, but even they would face trade-offs between basing within Chinese IRBM range on Guam or basing farther away in Alaska, Hawaii, or Australia. Ultimately, the United States would likely take a mixed approach. To generate enough combat power for the defense of Japan, at least some fighter aircraft might need to operate from Japan in wartime.

Bolstering Japan's missile defenses could require Japan to invest in (or the United States to provide) more-mobile systems for ballistic and cruise missile defense, especially sea-based systems, that would be less vulnerable to attack. Longer-range systems, including ASCMs, would allow Japan to intercept PLAN vessels before they could fire on Japan. Tokyo's cancellation in 2020 of the Aegis Ashore procurement does not bode well for investments in this area; however, Japan might invest more in these types of measures if the United States were to withdraw some or all of its military forces from Japan under a grand strategy of restraint.[50] Given the high cost of missile defense systems, Japan would need to balance these investments against other ways of improving its resiliency against missile attacks.

While some U.S. forces would need to remain in or near Japan to intervene in a timely manner, there are some forces currently stationed in the country that are not necessary for this type of scenario. For example, the United States could reduce its forces in Japan that support missions other than the defense of Japan itself. This mainly consists of the III Marine Expeditionary Force, which the United States stations on Okinawa but intends to deploy for contingencies involving the defense of South Korea or Taiwan.[51] Instead, the United States

---

[49] For an example of how U.S. ability to generate sorties—combat missions by individual aircraft—falls with distance, see Heginbotham et al., 2015, p. 80.

In theory, the United States could also consider basing in another country, such as the Philippines, but this seems like a less likely choice for advocates of restraint who might prefer to end the alliance with the Philippines. Basing in the Philippines would require a change to the Visiting Forces Agreement or rotational rather than permanently deployed forces (John Schaus, "What Is the Philippines–United States Visiting Forces Agreement, and Why Does It Matter?" Center for Strategic and International Studies, February 12, 2020).

[50] Hornung, 2020b; Hornung and Harold, 2021.

[51] III Marine Expeditionary Force, "III MEF Campaign Plan, 2015–2019," undated. III Marine Expeditionary Force is scheduled to relocate from Okinawa to Guam, Hawaii, the continental United States, and Australia in the mid-2020s. See Matthew M. Burke, "Marines' Move from Okinawa to Guam Could Begin as Early as October 2024, Report Says," *Stars and Stripes*, May 16, 2019.

would focus on crucial naval capabilities—carrier strike groups, destroyers, submarines, and logistics and resupply ships—and air assets necessary to defend the JSDF and to counter Chinese attacks on Japanese shipping.

The United States should further ensure that it has adequate protection and resiliency for operating bases, both for those in Japan hosting U.S. forces and for facilities in Guam, Australia, and other places. This includes maintaining the capability to distribute U.S. air and naval forces to a larger number of operating locations at the outset of conflict, hardening U.S. base infrastructure, and augmenting cyber defenses for U.S. forces and facilities.

The U.S. ability to defend Japan from Chinese attack also depends on Japan augmenting its own defenses and, in particular, on the resiliency and survivability of Japan's military forces and infrastructure. Security cooperation activities to support Japan's development of airpower and air and missile defense capabilities should be a high priority for restrainers. The JASDF should also continue investing in runway repair and other capabilities to provide additional resiliency against attacks on military airfields, stockpiling munitions and fuel, and hardening critical military infrastructure.[52]

Focusing less on amphibious capabilities and more on submarines, sealift, and airlift capabilities would allow Japan to mobilize or disperse its forces more quickly in the conflict. The JMSDF has an increasingly robust ASW capability that it should further augment given its importance to detecting and targeting Chinese naval forces and defending Japan's coastline and ports. Continued investment in longer-range ASCMs to offset the PLAN's missile range advantage would assist the JMSDF in holding Chinese forces at risk from farther away. To assist with the flow of forces and supplies during wartime, Japan could invest in port facilities that the JMSDF and U.S. Navy could access for logistics and supplies, and it could coordinate with the United States and Australia to use foreign ports, such as Guam or Perth, for maintenance or resupply in a conflict.[53] Furthermore, the United States should assist and encourage Japan to invest more in passive defenses and resiliency by hardening base and logistics infrastructure, better using camouflage and decoys, and procuring additional munitions and fuel reserves.[54]

Conclusion

Maintaining the JSDF as a force-in-being in the face of Chinese attacks, particularly given the PLA's quantitative and increasingly qualitative advantages over Japan, would likely require the United States to mobilize forces quickly once China expands its coercive campaign from

[52] Beckley, 2017.

[53] Hornung, 2020a, p. 54.

[54] Hornung, 2020a. For a general discussion of how these steps improve survivability, see Priebe et al., 2019; and Alan J. Vick and Mark Ashby, *Winning the Battle of the Airfields: Seventy Years of RAND Analysis on Air Base Defense and Attack*, Santa Monica, Calif.: RAND Corporation, RR-A793-1, 2021.

the Senkakus/Diaoyus to attacking the JSDF in other parts of Japan. Given the approximate timelines for the deployment of forces and the need to marshal forces quickly to counter China's attacks on the JSDF and Japan's coastline, we assess that the United States would need to have some naval forces present in or close to Japan at the outset of the conflict. The United States would not necessarily need to keep land-based air forces permanently stationed in the region during peacetime, but it would need to maintain air base access and have pre-positioned equipment and supplies. Future research should consider Japan's ability to defend its air and maritime space in the face of a Chinese attack and U.S. deployment timelines in more detail to make a more robust assessment. Beyond this, restrainers should consider security cooperation activities to help Japan increase its resiliency and capabilities for self-defense, which would allow more time for U.S. forces to arrive in the region and enable a smaller forward presence.

CHAPTER FOUR

After Occupying Taiwan, China Seizes the Southern Ryukyu Islands

Some analysts argue that gaining control of Taiwan would dramatically increase China's ability to project naval power into the Pacific Ocean and threaten Japan and other states in the region.[1] Restrainers generally would not fight to defend Taiwan, but many would be concerned about how China's occupation of the island would affect the security of Japan. This chapter examines how and why China might attack Japan after occupying Taiwan and positioning PLA forces there. In particular, we ask how China's control of Taiwan could shape its approach to seizing the southern Ryukyu Islands, the Japanese territory closest to Taiwan; what such a campaign might look like; and the implications for U.S. military requirements if a restraint-oriented United States wanted to be able to resist such aggression.

In this chapter, we examine a conflict over control of the southern Ryukyus that remains localized. Such a conflict could expand into a wider war like the one we discussed in Chapter Three, and it might not be clear at the outset of a conflict whether China's intentions were limited to the Ryukyus or whether it planned to pursue a more ambitious campaign against Japan. But, unlike with the first scenario, we are interested in understanding the U.S. military requirements to defend Japanese territory rather than to preserve the JSDF as a force-in-being, since these are different ways to conceptualize what it means to keep Japan as an independent security actor and because the kinds of campaigns that those objectives imply differ in important ways. Moreover, this scenario is an opportunity to evaluate the implications of Taiwan's fall for China's ability to invade rather than merely coerce its neighbors.

Our preliminary analysis suggests that the United States would need only a small forward-deployed military presence to achieve U.S. objectives in this scenario. We assess that China could seize islands in the southern Ryukyus very quickly given their proximity to Taiwan. Because the United States and Japan would likely fail to prevent China from seizing the islands initially, they would then focus on coercing China to give up the islands. Given such a

---

[1] Bonny Lin, "U.S. Allied and Partner Support for Taiwan: Responses to a Chinese Attack on Taiwan and Potential U.S. Taiwan Policy Changes," testimony presented before the U.S.-China Economic and Security Review Commission on February 18, 2021, Santa Monica, Calif.: RAND Corporation, CT-A1194-1, 2021, p. 4; Grant Newsham and Benjamin Self, "Resolved: Japan Should Deepen Defense/Security Cooperation with Japan," *Debating Japan*, Vol. 3, No. 3, April 2, 2020.

strategy, the United States would have time to deploy its air and naval forces into the region, which would then begin attriting Chinese forces as part of a cost-imposing strategy. Thus, a U.S. response would not be as urgent as in the scenario from Chapter Three, but some degree of speed would still be desirable to avoid either (1) the Chinese seizure of the islands becoming an established fait accompli or (2) the islands becoming bases for further Chinese attacks on Japan or an irresistible target that an unsupported JSDF might suffer heavy losses counterattacking. Having a small force charged with maintaining facilities and pre-positioned stocks in the region would allow the United States to respond in a timelier manner.

Scenario Context and Assumptions

This scenario envisions China moving beyond its claims to the Senkaku/Diaoyu Islands to assert claims to the central and southern islands in the Ryukyu island chain, which is the archipelago that extends southwest from Japan's home islands toward Taiwan. Okinawa, in the middle of the chain, is the largest of the Ryukyus and the location of major U.S. Air Force and Marine Corps bases.[2] While China has not made any formal claims on these islands, Chinese state-affiliated newspapers and think tanks have intermittently challenged Japan's legal claim to the Ryukyus.[3] In the hands of a less-than-friendly power, the islands pose a geographic barrier to Chinese naval forces seeking access to the Pacific Ocean from the East China Sea. Japanese ISR, anti-ship, and air defense capabilities on these islands can monitor or restrict the movement of Chinese vessels and naval forces through the Miyako Strait, a key choke point that runs between the islands of Miyako and Okinawa, connecting the East China and Philippine seas.[4] Gaining control of islands in the Ryukyus would help Chinese forces control the air and maritime space within the first island chain.[5] If China took control of Taiwan, it might develop a stronger interest than it has currently in controlling or neutralizing the southern Ryukyus because of their proximity to its newly acquired territory.

[2] Beckley, 2017, p. 96; Seth Cropsey, Jun Isomura, and James Conway, *U.S.-Japan Cooperation on Strategic Island Defense*, Washington, D.C.: Hudson Institute, 2018, p. 8; Hornung, 2020a.

[3] The Chinese government refers to this as *scholarly debate* and emphasizes that it is not official policy (Jane Perlez, "Calls Grow in China to Press Claim for Okinawa," *New York Times*, June 13, 2013). This challenge focuses on a historical tributary relationship between the Ryukyu Kingdom and the Qing dynasty. See Gordon C. Chang, "Now China Wants Okinawa, Site of U.S. Bases in Japan," *Daily Beast*, last updated June 26, 2017; and Chun Han Wong, "China Affirms Japan Sovereignty over Okinawa, Ryukyu Islands," *Wall Street Journal*, June 2, 2013. One potential reason for the unofficial dispute over the Ryukyus is to generate bargaining leverage in negotiations over the Senkakus/Diaoyus (Chang, 2017; Justin McCurry, "China Lays Claim to Okinawa as Territory Dispute with Japan Escalates," *The Guardian*, May 15, 2013).

[4] Cropsey, Isomura, and Conway, 2018, p. 12.

[5] Yoshihara, 2020a. The PLA regularly transits the straits between the Ryukyus during peacetime. See Cropsey, Isomura, and Conway, 2018, p. 17; and Tetsuo Kotani, "China's Military and Paramilitary Activities in the East China Sea: Trends and Assessments for the U.S.-Japan Alliance," *Asia Policy*, Vol. 15, No. 3, July 2020, p. 12.

Stationing forces on the islands and controlling the air and maritime space around them would provide an additional layer of security for China's presence on and around Taiwan and remove a potential obstacle to projecting power from it.

The focus of this scenario is a Chinese military seizure of the Sakishima Islands (Figure 4.1), which is the portion of the Ryukyus closest to Taiwan. The total population of these islands is approximately 110,000 people. The vast majority of the civilian population is concentrated on two of the largest islands, Ishigaki and Miyako (Table 4.1).

For this scenario, we assume that China seized Taiwan in the mid-2020s in a surprise attack that resulted in minimal losses to the invaders, so the PLA's capabilities remained largely intact, and that it has deployed substantial forces to occupy and defend the island, including long-range rocket artillery, SRBMs, attack helicopters, ASCM-armed fast attack craft, and a multilayer integrated air defense system. We also assume that the United States did not intervene militarily to defend Taiwan. In the several years following the invasion,

FIGURE 4.1

The Southern Ryukyu Islands

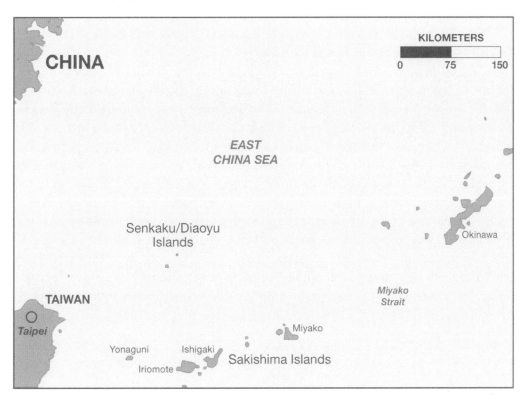

TABLE 4.1

The Largest Sakishima Islands

Island	Area (km²)	Population	Distance from Taiwan (km)	Distance from Okinawa (km)
Yonaguni	29	1,500	115	505
Iriomote	289	2,400	205	430
Ishigaki	223	48,900	230	405
Miyako	159	47,700	335	280

SOURCES: Population and area are from Visit Okinawa Japan, "Miyako Region," webpage, undated a; and Visit Okinawa Japan, "Yaeyama Region," webpage, undated b.
NOTES: Population figures were calculated by adding population figures from the description of each island linked at the two webpages cited. Distances are approximations based on Google Maps measurements to each island's main population center from the nearest coastline of Taiwan or Okinawa.

Japan strengthened the JSDF and increased its military presence in Okinawa and in the Sakishimas because of their vulnerability to PLA forces operating from Taiwan.[6]

China now seeks to gain control over the Sakishima Islands because of the advantages that this offers for power projection from Taiwan and to eliminate the possibility that Japan or the United States could use the islands as bases from which to undermine Chinese control of Taiwan. Beijing believes that Japan will not cede part of its homeland, even under strong coercive pressure, so it decides to take the islands by force.

For counterhegemonic restrainers, these islands are worth defending either because they are part of Japan, which is a critical ally for balancing against China, or because they are strategic territory that helps limit China's ability to project power into the Pacific. Defensive restrainers would likely consider the Sakishimas to be both indefensible and not vital enough to U.S. interests to justify the risk of war with China—like Taiwan, but without the defensive advantages that the larger Taiwanese population and territory provide. Flexible restrainers may share this concern about the strength of Japan's defensive position in the Sakishimas but nevertheless support using force because Chinese aggression against territories beyond Taiwan would suggest much more malign intentions than restrainers currently attribute to China. An unprovoked attack on Japan would represent (or reveal) a turn in China's overall behavior toward a belligerent, malign, and revisionist path, which would run counter to the beliefs among some within the restraint community that China is not particularly expansionist.[7] China's aggressive behavior might raise concerns that, if unchecked,

---

[6] Stephen Stashwick, "Japan Confirms New Missile Deployments to Ryukyu Islands," *The Diplomat*, August 6, 2021. We do not assume that, by this point, Japan has transformed the Sakishimas into fortified redoubts; a desire to strike before Japan hardens them more extensively might play a substantial role in China's decision to attack so soon after the fall of Taiwan.

[7] Restrainers understand that China seeks reunification with Taiwan. These strategists are unsure of China's territorial ambitions beyond Taiwan and China's willingness to take risks to fulfill them. Aggression against Japan would show that China's intentions had become more far-ranging than many restrainers had previously assessed. It is possible, of course, that a restraint-oriented U.S. government would recalibrate its

Beijing will attempt to take additional territory in the future. This scenario therefore posits that the United States decides to intervene on Japan's behalf. We also assume, however, that the restraint-oriented U.S. government does not want to escalate the conflict by threatening China's control of the population on Taiwan or striking targets in mainland China.

Although we focus on the military dimensions of this scenario, we assume that the United States and Japan would also exert diplomatic pressure on allies and partners around the world to introduce economic measures to punish China, such as sanctions against Chinese companies or restrictions on PRC shipping and overseas port access, to further heighten the cost of the conflict. This Chinese attack on Japanese territory, particularly in the wake of the seizure of Taiwan, would presumably result in considerable international condemnation, which would make it easier to mobilize such an effort. Chapter Five addresses how the United States could combine economic sanctions with a military blockade of China as part of a larger cost-imposing strategy.[8]

PLA Approach to Seizing the Southern Ryukyus

China's goal in this scenario is to gain and maintain control of the Sakishimas themselves and the air and maritime space around the islands. Operationally, China would focus on first taking the southernmost islands, which would help it gain control of the air and maritime space by preventing Japanese missile forces on these islands from targeting PLA ships and aircraft.

China's approach would likely rely on a brief missile, rocket, and air attack to disable the islands' air defense and anti-ship missile systems and other forces that Japan may have deployed to the islands following China's seizure of Taiwan. The PLA would follow this attack by sending airborne, air assault, and amphibious forces from Taiwan to land on the islands and take over airfields and other military or critical civilian infrastructure, under an umbrella of fighter and SAM cover to prevent effective interference by Japanese or U.S. airpower. The PLAN and PLAAF would deploy aircraft, surface ships, and submarines to patrol the waters and airspace around the islands and to restrict any Japanese attempts to support the JSDF forces stationed on them, in addition to isolating the civilian population residing on the islands. The PLA's position on Taiwan, located roughly as close to the islands as Taiwan is to the Chinese mainland (approximately 160 km), would enable both (1) sustained ISR for targeting Japanese capabilities and (2) the rapid movement of PLA forces and supplies quickly from Taiwan to the Sakishimas.

threat perceptions about China following an invasion of Taiwan and decide at that point to increase U.S. force presence in Japan or the Western Pacific more generally as a deterrent measure, although this scenario does not assume such a posture shift.

[8] Global support for economic sanctions on Russia following its invasion of Ukraine in 2022 reinforce this prediction.

After gaining control of the islands, the PLA would use Taiwan-based fighters and MPA, SAM batteries on Taiwan, PLAN surface ships equipped with SAMs and ASCMs, and attack submarines to control the surrounding air and maritime space. This control would enable China to threaten the JMSDF and to defend the islands from counterattacks. The PLAN would also likely fly MPA based in Taiwan to hunt for Japanese submarines and would likely deploy its own submarines on ASW patrols. The PLA could then deploy surface-to-surface missiles and SAMs on any islands that it had captured to augment the A2/AD umbrella from its forces at sea and on Taiwan. Moreover, the missile forces on both mainland China and Taiwan can reach the entire archipelago, which would enable the PLA to hold Japanese maritime and air capabilities near the southern Ryukyus at risk and to attack Japan's military infrastructure on Okinawa.[9]

It is unclear how China would deal with the civilian population on the Ryukyus. On the one hand, the presence of Japanese civilians on the seized islands would be a powerful motivation for Japan to continue fighting to retake the islands.[10] In addition, the presence of a sizable civilian population that is hostile to China would be a drain on PLA resources and require additional supplies on top of the occupation demands related to Taiwan. China would, therefore, have some reasons to offer to repatriate the citizens as an incentive for Japan to agree to a cease-fire. On the other hand, China might prefer not to relocate civilians whose presence could discourage Japanese strikes against targets on the occupied islands.

Japanese and U.S. Approaches

Although the JSDF has made some improvements to defenses of the southern Ryukyu Islands, including deploying air defense and anti-ship missile batteries on several of them, they are still not as well defended as Okinawa or the Japanese home islands.[11] As we discuss below, there are additional steps that Japan could take to make these islands harder to seize, and we assume that Japan would try to do so following the invasion of Taiwan or even before. Even with such investments, China could likely take the islands quickly with little additional military mobilization given their proximity to Taiwan and the capabilities that the PLA would likely have deployed there. Therefore, in this scenario, we consider the possibility that Japan and the United States would have little warning time to react prior to China's actions. Because it is unlikely that the United States and Japan could prevent Chinese conquest of the islands, U.S. and Japanese objectives would focus on regaining control of the islands by making it prohibitively costly for China to hold them. At the same time, the United States and Japan would

---

[9]   For Chinese SRBM and IRBM ranges, see Defense Intelligence Ballistic Missile Analysis Committee, 2020, pp. 21, 25.

[10]   The civilian population of the Falkland Islands when Argentina invaded them in 1982 numbered fewer than 2,000 (Martin Middlebrook, *The Falklands War, 1982*, New York: Penguin, 2001).

[11]   Stashwick, 2021.

need to counter Chinese attacks on Japanese and U.S. forces, as well as deter further Chinese aggression. The United States and Japan would also seek to ensure the safety of the civilian population on the islands as a subsidiary goal.

A restraint-oriented United States likely would not pursue an assault to retake the islands. Amphibious assaults on these islands could lead to large numbers of casualties, and, once U.S. forces were ashore, they would be vulnerable to air and missile attacks from Taiwan and mainland China. The preferred U.S. military strategy would focus on imposing costs on the Chinese forces occupying the islands with the goal of compelling a Chinese withdrawal. The Japanese government, however, would be keen to liberate the islands once it had reduced the PLA forces on and around them to the point that counterattacks were feasible.[12] Therefore, Japan might conduct amphibious assaults to retake the islands, even at the risk of large numbers of casualties, while U.S. forces would likely have the more limited role of supporting the Japanese counterattack with air and maritime attacks against the Chinese forces.

To make China's occupation of the islands untenable, the United States and Japan would need to degrade Chinese control of the air and maritime space around the islands. This would allow U.S. and Japanese forces to deny China the ability to resupply its forces on the islands and would make it difficult for China to send reinforcements to replace losses among the occupying forces. To accomplish this, the United States and Japan would focus on isolating the islands by holding at risk Chinese ships and aircraft attempting to sustain the PLA forces on the islands, using aircraft and submarines to target Chinese ships and aircraft on resupply missions or patrolling the waters and airspace around the islands. If Japan invests in longer-range ASCMs and bases them on Okinawa or other islands in the Ryukyu archipelago, it could also use those against PLAN forces. To intercept aerial resupply of the islands by helicopters and fixed-wing transports, and to deter Chinese use of ASW aircraft in the vicinity, the United States and Japan would use advanced fighter aircraft that can more safely operate within the reach of PLA fighters and SAM batteries on Taiwan than other aircraft. U.S. and Japanese surface ships would be vulnerable to attack if they sailed close to the islands or near Taiwan, but some would be able to fire on Chinese forces from outside the range of Chinese ASCMs.[13] In addition, to supplement U.S. ISR, Japan could use ISR capabilities from the JASDF, which could include the deployment of UAVs and unmanned underwater vehicles, to detect and target Chinese forces.

In the absence of other coercive measures, such as attacks on Chinese targets elsewhere or a blockade of China (see Chapter Five), it seems unlikely that simply trying to starve out the occupation forces in the Sakishimas would persuade China to withdraw them. In addition, doing so would cause the Japanese civilian populace on the islands to starve. U.S. and Japa-

---

[12] Japan Ministry of Defense, 2020a, pp. 261–262.

[13] China's longest-range air-launched ASCM, the YJ-12, has a range of 300–400 km, while the YJ-18, the PLAN's newest submarine-launched ASCM, has a range of 220 km. A RAND report from 2015 assessed that the U.S. Navy would maintain an advantage over the PLAN in anti-ship missile defense capabilities and could target PLAN ships from greater distances than these (Heginbotham et al., 2015, pp. 171–184, 215–219).

nese forces would therefore attempt to isolate PLA forces on the islands, so that reinforcing the garrison would be challenging, and would then seek to attrit the existing Chinese forces on the islands. This would primarily rely on precision air and missile attacks launched from outside the main PLA air defense umbrella. Attacking PLA air defense systems deployed on the islands would be a priority, since degrading these capabilities would facilitate subsequent strikes on other targets.[14] Collecting targeting intelligence on these forces from a variety of sources would be critical.

Finally, attacking long-range SAMs in northeastern Taiwan might be necessary to maintain the U.S. and Japanese fighter presence required to reliably intercept low-altitude resupply flights from Taiwan to the Sakishimas. Advocates of restraint would likely try to avoid striking targets on Taiwan—which China would consider its own territory—particularly given that China has not broadened its military operations beyond the southern Ryukyu Islands. However, air and missile attacks launched from Taiwan might convince the United States that treating Taiwan as a sanctuary is untenable. Because China has taken Japanese territory, Japan would presumably be even more motivated to strike targets on Taiwan.

Implications for U.S. Posture and Force Structure

In this scenario, we assume that China intends to keep the conflict over the Ryukyus limited. As we noted at the outset of this chapter, U.S. policymakers could not know this in advance with certainty, and a fight for control of the southern Ryukyus could easily expand. Therefore, restrainers concerned with the defense of Japan might prefer to plan for a peacetime posture and wartime deployments that would also enable the United States to defend the JSDF against widespread Chinese attacks (see Chapter Three). This section offers insights for (1) restrainers who want the United States to be able to respond to both an attack on the Ryukyus and attacks on the JSDF and (2) restrainers who believe that such a conflict could stay limited. The distinction between defense of territory and preservation of the JSDF as a force-in-being is important because the former might generate requirements for capabilities or capacity levels that are different from the latter. That is, while defending the Ryukyus has the potential to escalate into a broader coercive campaign, defending specific territory can still create implications for U.S. posture on top of those outlined in Chapter Three, or the United States might believe that it could face a scenario that requires only preserving Japanese territorial integrity rather than defending Japan's armed forces more generally.

When it comes to an attack on the Sakishimas, the United States would not need to respond to the aggression immediately; compelling China to withdraw from the Sakishimas would presumably take sustained effort, and Japan would retain considerable capabilities to

---

[14] The United States and Japan might be interested in delivering some supplies to the islands' residents via precision airdrop to help sustain the civilian populace, but this would be difficult to do successfully on small islands under the eyes of substantial occupation forces, even setting aside issues of air defense.

defend its home islands in the near term.[15] This means that the United States would not necessarily need to have forces deployed forward in Japan or elsewhere in the Western Pacific to respond specifically to an attack on the Sakishimas (although it might want to respond quickly to augment the defense of the rest of the Japan). At the same time, a military intervention against Chinese forces on the Sakishimas would need to be reasonably prompt, so having infrastructure and pre-positioned supplies in Japan or other operating locations would be important to ensure that U.S. forces could quickly initiate and sustain combat operations when they arrive. Having sufficient lift capacity to bring forces and materiel in from outside the region would also be essential. At least a small number of U.S. forces, likely from the U.S. Army, would remain in Japan during peacetime to manage facilities and pre-positioned supplies.[16] Should China not capitulate quickly, the United States might need to sustain its forces and operations for months.

Given the allied approach of striking the Chinese forces on the Sakishimas and interdicting their resupply and reinforcement, the United States would rely heavily on land- and sea-based airpower, including fighters that could intercept PLAAF aircraft and helicopters, fighters or bombers with precision weapons for strikes against the occupation forces, and aircraft with anti-ship weapons to attack naval forces and cargo vessels (including ones too small to be engaged by submarines cost-effectively). These strike assets would depend in turn on manned and unmanned ISR aircraft and other sensors to provide surveillance of the air and maritime space around the Ryukyus and on tanker support to sustain operations at long ranges from U.S. bases or carriers. Maintaining combat air patrols in the vicinity of the islands would be demanding for U.S. and Japanese forces, but merely periodic presence would be inadequate to isolate the islands because, when the fighters were not on station, resupply flights from Taiwan could deliver attrition replacements and additional materiel to the PLA garrisons.

The United States could conduct air and missile strikes against Chinese forces on the islands at times that were convenient for it and its Japanese counterparts. Besides avoiding or suppressing Chinese air defenses, the main challenge in this aspect of the campaign would be targeting PLA forces without causing Japanese civilian casualties, which would likely be a major concern for Tokyo and which Chinese forces would presumably make as difficult as possible. This would place a premium on standoff weapons with small warheads designed to minimize collateral damage.[17] It would also be essential to be able to draw on the kinds

---

[15] As we noted at the beginning of the chapter, if the United States worried that Chinese war aims might quickly expand beyond the southern Ryukyus, it would want to have forces to protect against a Chinese attack on Japan's military or economy (Chapter Three).

[16] The Army currently performs this role in Japan (U.S. Forces, Japan, "Guidance from the Commander, U.S. Forces Japan," webpage, undated).

[17] See Becca Wasser, Stacie L. Pettyjohn, Jeffrey Martini, Alexandra T. Evans, Karl P. Mueller, Nathaniel Edenfield, Gabrielle Tarini, Ryan Haberman, and Jalen Zeman, *The Air War Against the Islamic State: The Role of Airpower in Operation Inherent Resolve*, Santa Monica, Calif.: RAND Corporation, RR-A388-1, 2021.

and scale of intelligence-processing and analytical targeting capabilities that exist in U.S. air operations centers for planning effective attacks while limiting risks to civilians.[18]

As in the previous scenario, the United States would face trade-offs in deciding where to base its aircraft. Tactical aircraft based in Japan prior to the conflict or deployed there after it began would have a relatively high sortie rate and would require less in-flight refueling than aircraft operating from locations farther from China, such as Guam, Australia, or Alaska, but their bases would be more vulnerable to PLA missile attack and would require U.S. investments in hardening base facilities and pre-positioning materiel and munitions. U.S. aircraft carrier operations would confront the same trade-off with respect to whether to operate inside or outside the threat rings of Chinese ASBMs. These considerations would make long-range bombers attractive for many counterland and countersea missions. To use these bombers at scale, the United States would need to maintain a large stockpile of munitions. UAVs capable of operating from non–air base locations might be well suited to some of these roles if the U.S. Air Force acquired that capability at a large enough scale.[19] In addition to airpower, the United States and Japan would want to use submarines to interdict larger Chinese surface ships ferrying supplies and reinforcements to the Ryukyus and to target PLAN forces providing air defense or maritime control around the islands. The number of submarines in the U.S. 7th Fleet currently ranges between eight and 12 in peacetime, operating from Hawaii and Guam.[20] Given the 2021 security agreement between the United States, the United Kingdom, and Australia, U.S. attack submarines might also be able to operate from HMAS Stirling in Western Australia by the time this conflict scenario occurs. Additional submarine tenders—the U.S. Navy currently has only two, one located at Guam—would expand options for submarine basing at other locations. China will have also deployed submarines around the Ryukyus, but the U.S. Navy currently retains a significant edge over the PLAN in ASW capabilities and undersea warfare, making this an area of U.S. comparative advantage.[21]

The United States would require numerous logistics ships and tankers to support tactical air and naval operations and to resupply JSDF forces when needed. The United States could base some of these assets in Japan, particularly if it decided to maintain a limited air or naval presence there. However, it would presumably want to have most of these capabilities based

---

[18] Sherrill Lingel, Jeff Hagen, Eric Hastings, Mary Lee, Matthew Sargent, Matthew Walsh, Li Ang Zhang, and David Blancett, *Joint All-Domain Command and Control for Modern Warfare: An Analytic Framework for Identifying and Developing Artificial Intelligence Applications*, Santa Monica, Calif.: RAND Corporation, RR-4408/1-AF, 2020, pp. 34–39.

[19] Thomas Hamilton and David Ochmanek, *Operating Low-Cost, Reusable Unmanned Aerial Vehicles in Contested Environments: Preliminary Evaluation of Operational Concepts*, Santa Monica, Calif.: RAND Corporation, RR-4407-AF, 2020.

[20] Commander, U.S. 7th Fleet, "The United States Seventh Fleet," webpage, undated.

[21] Heginbotham et al., 2015, pp. 208–214. On the longer-term challenges potentially facing the U.S. submarine force as China's ASW capabilities improve, see Bryan Clark, *The Emerging Era in Undersea Warfare*, Washington, D.C.: Center for Strategic and Budgetary Assessments, January 22, 2015.

farther away, especially in wartime, potentially in Guam or Australia, where they would be less vulnerable to Chinese attack than if they were based in the region.[22]

There are several areas where Japan would have to make additional investments if U.S. forces in Japan were to draw down, especially after the fall of Taiwan. These include deploying additional SAMs, ASCMs, and other defensive forces; stockpiling munitions in the southern Ryukyus; and strengthening JSDF capabilities on Okinawa.[23] Such steps could enhance deterrence by raising the costs of a Chinese attack. At the very least, such steps could make a Chinese attack slower and more difficult, giving Japan more time to respond before attacks on other islands begin. Although Japan has a robust minesweeper capability, it could invest more in mines, which would further inhibit PLA forces from operating in the littoral waters, harbors, or ports on these islands.[24] On the Sakishimas and on the rest of the Ryukyus, increasing the resilience and hardening of the Japanese forces deployed there and their supporting logistics and infrastructure would be useful because of China's ability to reach these islands with extensive missile and air capabilities. This includes encouraging Japan to invest in capabilities—such as jamming and electronic warfare capabilities, including counterspace capabilities—to undermine Chinese ISR and targeting systems that can target Japan's mobile ASCMs and SAMs. Japan could also increase stockpiles of munitions and other supplies that it would need to sustain operations during a long conflict.

Conclusion

China's occupation of Taiwan and the fact that the PLA can deploy substantial missile, naval, and air capabilities there would allow Chinese forces to rapidly seize the Sakishima Islands and to establish local air and maritime control around them. The U.S. response would benefit from forward-deployed tactical air forces and associated logistics capabilities that the United States could quickly marshal from bases in Japan and deploy at high sortie rates, and the United States could supplement these by bringing in air and naval forces from locations farther away. Alternatively, the United States could completely rely on forces operating from locations farther away, including Guam, Hawaii, Alaska, and potentially Australia; however, this would affect the sortie rate for U.S. aircraft and the U.S. ability to contest China's air control around the islands.

---

[22] Currently, 7th Fleet has 50 combat logistics ships commanded from Singapore (Commander, U.S. 7th Fleet, undated).

[23] Japan has already deployed two batteries each of ASCMs and SAMs to the Ryukyus with plans to deploy a third and to procure longer-range versions of these systems. The current Type-12 ASCM has a range of 200 km, and the Type-03 SAM has a range of 50 km and engagement altitude of 10,000 m (Hornung, 2020a, pp. 65–66; Tim Kelly, "Japan to Develop Longer-Range Anti-Ship Missiles as China Pressure Mounts," Reuters, December 18, 2020).

[24] Jim Hartman, "The United States and Japan Still Benefit from Complementary Maritime Capabilities," *War on the Rocks*, March 9, 2021.

The United States would also require logistics support, likely from outside Japan, that could resupply U.S. and Japanese forces for months if the conflict became a protracted war of attrition. On Japan's part, investments in augmenting air and missile defenses in the Ryukyus, hardening facilities and bases there, and enhancing capabilities that could target Chinese ISR would be especially useful in defending the islands, or at least making it more difficult and costly for the PLA to seize the most-vulnerable ones.

CHAPTER FIVE

The United States Imposes a Distant Blockade on China During a War Between China and Japan

For our third scenario, we consider the possibility that the United States might impose a coercive maritime blockade against China. The United States might do this if it were willing to bear some costs and risks to counter Chinese aggression but unwilling to escalate to more-direct operations against the PLA. Such a campaign could be one element of a larger war to defend Japan or to protect any other vital interest. A distant blockade at maritime choke points, such as the Strait of Malacca, would take advantage of U.S. strengths in naval power projection and exploit China's economic reliance on maritime trade, especially for imports of crude oil. If the blockade succeeded at imposing substantial economic punishment on China, it would contribute to a broader coercive strategy designed to build pressure to end a conflict on terms acceptable to the United States.

After considering such a blockade in more detail, we find that it meshes well with the logic of restraint insofar as it does not require a large onshore U.S. military presence in the Asia-Pacific during peacetime. However, to impose and sustain a blockade to the point at which it would inflict severe enough economic damage on China, the United States would need to maintain a large surface fleet at home, deploy a sizable portion of it to the region during the conflict, and establish agreements with other countries in the region to use ports and military facilities that could sustain U.S. operations over a long period.

Blockading China outside the context of an ongoing major conflict would impose serious economic costs on the United States and the global economy, and, although the risks of escalation to a broader conflict would certainly be lower than those of a campaign involving widespread strikes on the Chinese mainland, they would still be significant. These costs and risks might be incommensurate with the limited interests that restrainers perceive to be at stake in many regional scenarios. However, if the United States were already fighting China, including a blockade in the U.S. strategy would entail smaller marginal costs and risks because a U.S.-Chinese war would already be disrupting bilateral trade.

Because of the challenges that the United States would have to overcome to make it effective, a blockade of China would not be a panacea. Although China's peacetime import dependence is considerable, it would have a variety of tools to undermine a blockade's effectiveness. In the case of a blockade of maritime oil and gas imports, the focus of discussion later in this chapter, these tools include rationing domestic fuel consumption, drawing on strategic reserves, adding fuel extenders, increasing overland oil imports, attacking U.S. forces involved in the blockade, imposing retaliatory economic or military costs on the United States, and pressuring third parties to withdraw their support for the presumably lengthy coercive effort.[1] China would not need all of these countermeasures to work well—it would only need enough goods to get past the U.S. blockade to match supply with critical demand.[2] Because China can implement such countermeasures, it is very unlikely that a blockade would quickly result in Chinese concessions.

Scenario Context

For this scenario, we consider the use of a distant blockade against China in the context of a war between China and Japan. There is more than one way that the United States could use a blockade during such a war. The United States might use a coercive blockade as an alternative response to China seizing the southern Ryukyu Islands (see Chapter Four). In this case, the United States would attempt to use the blockade to compel China to withdraw without suffering the losses and running the escalatory risks associated with directly attacking the Chinese forces controlling the islands. Another blockade narrative builds on the campaign of attacks against Japan from Chapter Three. In this variant, the United States directly intervenes in response to Chinese aggression to prevent the elimination of Japan as an effective air and naval power. Because defending Japan without decisively eliminating the PLA threat appears likely to lead to a protracted and costly conflict that might drag on as long as China is willing to continue it, the United States also imposes a distant blockade against China to increase the compellent pressure on Beijing.[3]

In either case, a blockade would be part of a larger campaign to inflict economic punishment on China as a coercive lever. A broader diplomatic effort would seek to incentivize and coerce other states to limit their trade and other economic ties with China, such as by embargoing energy exports. A heavy reliance on the diplomatic component of this campaign is consistent with restrainers' preference for relying on nonmilitary tools more than on military means when possible. As we describe in later sections, imposing a sustained blockade would be demanding on the U.S. military, so the effort would benefit from any steps that would

---

[1] For all of these reasons, strategists should not imagine that a blockade of oil imports or other strategic materials would be a useful course of action for compelling China to cease an activity occurring over a relatively short timeline, such as an invasion of Taiwan, by depriving the PLA of fuel or other resources.

[2] Gabriel B. Collins, "A Maritime Oil Blockade Against China—Tactically Tempting but Strategically Flawed," *Naval War College Review*, Vol. 71, No. 2, Spring 2018, p. 52.

[3] On contests of coercion, see Daniel Byman and Matthew Waxman, *The Dynamics of Coercion: American Foreign Policy and the Limits of Military Might*, Cambridge, United Kingdom: Cambridge University Press, 2002.

reduce the number of vessels to inspect or monitor. The easiest way to disrupt trade is to prevent others from loading ships with exports bound for China in the first place. The United States would develop a punishment and reward system to support the blockade through non-military means, but it would also face a comparable Chinese effort, which might have better leverage over some countries whose economies depend heavily on trade with China. In short, consistent with the logic of restraint, the United States would rely as heavily as possible on diplomatic and economic means to protect its interests, hoping to minimize the amount of military force necessary to achieve its ends.

Given the context, discussed above, of an ongoing conflict with China over Japan, we assess that the United States would impose a distant blockade at maritime choke points far from China's shores rather than a close blockade in its immediate littoral waters, which would significantly raise the risks of escalation and threat to U.S. forces.[4] A distant blockade would take advantage of the Asia-Pacific's geography, which funnels China-bound merchant shipping through narrow choke points that are accessible to U.S. naval forces (Figure 5.1). More than 70 percent of Chinese oil imports normally transit the Strait of Malacca from the Indian Ocean into the South China Sea during peacetime, although China could use alternative routes through the Indonesian archipelago that would add four to 16 days of transit time and millions of dollars per day in shipping costs.[5] Military personnel from U.S. surface ships would board and inspect merchant vessels in Southeast Asia near the Malacca, Sunda, and Lombok Straits and in the Solomon Sea to cover the alternative trade route around Australia.[6] U.S. forces in the Middle East might also support the blockade in the Arabian Sea or at the Strait of Hormuz, through which around 40 percent of China's maritime oil imports pass.[7]

To inform this scenario, we drew on historical examples of blockades, including the United Nations (UN) maritime coalition campaign to enforce sanctions on Iraq during and after the 1991 Gulf War, in which coalition naval forces conducted visit, board, search, and seizure (VBSS) operations in the Persian Gulf, the Gulf of Oman, and the Red Sea.[8] The

---

[4] On the distinctions and trade-offs between a distant and close blockade, see Mirski, 2013; and Evan Braden Montgomery, "Reconsidering a Naval Blockade of China: A Response to Mirski," *Journal of Strategic Studies*, Vol. 36, No. 4, 2013. We consider only a distant blockade because restrainers interested in limiting escalation risks might be uncomfortable with the risks to U.S. forces from Chinese missiles and attacks by PLA aircraft and naval forces should the United States implement a blockade closer to the Chinese mainland.

[5] Center for Strategic and International Studies, "How Much Trade Transits the South China Sea?" last updated January 25, 2021; Collins, 2018, p. 86; Office of the Secretary of Defense, *Annual Report to Congress: Military and Security Developments Involving the People's Republic of China 2019*, Washington, D.C.: Department of Defense, May 2, 2019, p. 12.

[6] Collins, 2018, pp. 54–55; Cunningham, 2020, p. 752. If Indonesia or Malaysia provides access, U.S. ground forces could also support a blockade by sending boarding teams on small boats and helicopters.

[7] Bonnie Girard, "China and Gulf Security: Conspicuous by Its Absence," *The Diplomat*, May 7, 2020.

[8] Michael R. Gordon, "Confrontation in the Gulf: Navy Begins Blockade Enforcing Iraq Embargo," *New York Times*, August 17, 1990. In response to Iraq's invasion of Kuwait in 1990, the UN Security Council

blockade supported a broader diplomatic campaign to pressure countries to stop trading with Iraq and involved VBSS operations to interdict merchant vessels with minimal force and to distinguish between blockade-runners (that is, ships trying to evade the blockade to reach Iraq) and neutral trade bound for third parties.[9]

FIGURE 5.1

Maritime Choke Points for Shipping from the Indian Ocean to China

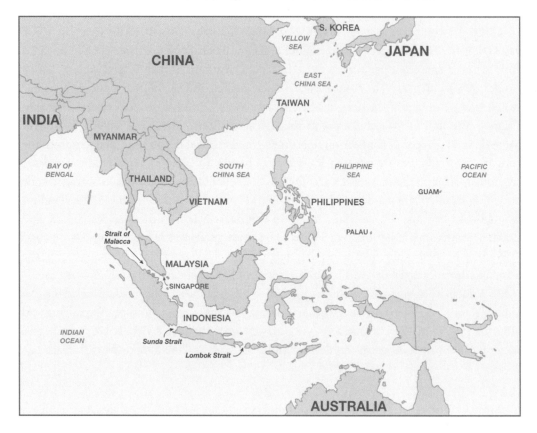

imposed comprehensive sanctions on Iraq, which would continue after the war. These included bans on imports and exports and freezes on Iraq's foreign assets (Peter Wallensteen, Carina Staibano, and Mikael Eriksson, *The 2004 Roundtable on UN Sanctions Against Iraq: Lessons Learned*, Uppsala, Sweden: Uppsala University, 2005, pp. 5–6).

[9] James Gerstenzang, "Willing to Blockade Iraq to Stop Any Oil Shipment, Bush Says: Sanctions: But the President Reports That the U.N. Embargo Has Virtually Halted World Trade with Baghdad," *Los Angeles Times*, August 12, 1990.

U.S. Military Approach to a Distant Blockade

As we discuss below, conducting a blockade would be very demanding for the U.S. Navy. The United States could not board and search every ship and would therefore need to set enforcement priorities. We assume that the United States would focus on halting China's oil and liquified natural gas imports by sea, although it could also interdict other merchant shipping.[10] China would be vulnerable to a blockade targeting its oil resources. It is the world's largest importer of crude oil, which it imports at a rate of more than 10 million bpd to satisfy 70 percent of its oil demand.[11] Furthermore, oil and gas tankers are relatively easy to differentiate from dry bulk cargo and container ships, and there are fewer of them, so limiting the focus of a blockade to interdicting oil and gas shipments to China would dramatically reduce the military requirements of such an operation.[12]

Because even an exceptionally successful blockade would not completely sever China's access to energy supplies, we assume that the blockade would not deny China the ability to achieve its military objectives during a regional war by starving the PLA of the resources it would need to sustain its ongoing operations. China could ration domestic fuel supplies for nonessential purposes and lean on overland imports of oil, so it would take a long time—at least months and potentially years—for the blockade to generate enough damage to seriously constrain PLA operations.[13] Instead, the U.S. strategy would hinge on damaging the Chinese economy and demonstrating the U.S. ability to threaten China's access to energy resources as a means to pressure the Chinese government to end the conflict.

To implement the blockade, the United States would rely on surface ships at distant choke points to board and inspect merchant ships, interdict blockade-runners, and grant safe passage to neutral trade. The U.S. Navy would take on the lion's share of the responsibility for enforcing a blockade by providing surface ships with helicopters and boarding teams for VBSS operations and MPA and UAV squadrons for the surveillance and targeting of Chinese forces responding to the blockade. The U.S. Coast Guard could provide additional vessels and personnel with institutional knowledge based on extensive experience with coastal

---

[10] The United States could attempt to interdict all of China's seaborne trade, or some specific set of goods beyond oil and gas, but we concentrate our attention on the requirements for a blockade focused exclusively on China's energy imports. This follows most of the existing literature on a potential U.S. blockade of China and makes the requirements more feasible (Collins, 2018; Collins and Murray, 2008; Andrew Erickson and Gabriel B. Collins, "Beijing's Energy Security Strategy: The Significance of a Chinese State-Owned Tanker Fleet," *Orbis*, Vol. 51, No. 4, Fall 2007; Andrew Erickson and Gabriel Collins, "China's Oil Security Pipe Dream—The Reality, and Strategic Consequences, of Seaborne Imports," *Naval War College Review*, Vol. 63, No. 2, Spring 2010; Llewelyn Hughes and Austin Long, "Is There an Oil Weapon? Security Implications of Changes in the Structure of the International Oil Market," *International Security*, Vol. 39, No. 3, Winter 2014–2015; Lind and Press, 2018).

[11] Nathaniel Taplin, "China Is Approaching Its Own Peak Oil," *Wall Street Journal*, February 12, 2021.

[12] Jason Glab, "Blockading China: A Guide," *War on the Rocks*, October 1, 2013.

[13] Collins, 2018.

interdiction operations. Other U.S. military services would also contribute. For example, the U.S. Marine Corps and Army could provide boarding teams. The U.S. Air Force could operate manned and unmanned aircraft from Guam and potentially Australia, Japan, or other locations in the region, depending on which nations were actively supporting the blockade. These aircraft would help protect the airspace around the blockade's task groups, support maritime domain awareness, pursue blockade-runners, or threaten Chinese forces escorting ships. U.S. satellites would monitor maritime traffic at Chinese ports, which would help identify blockade-runners that U.S. forces could later interdict, and both aerial and space-based surveillance would monitor tanker traffic throughout the region. Finally, the broader sanctions regime would require the support of significant civilian infrastructure that would include participation from the U.S. Intelligence Community, State Department, and Treasury Department.

A central challenge for the United States would be differentiating blockade-runners from legitimate neutral shipping.[14] This would not be as simple as interdicting Chinese-flagged vessels while allowing others to pass.[15] China could use flags of convenience and forgery to conceal a ship's intended destination, and a neutral-flagged vessel headed for a neutral port could change its destination and deliver its cargo to China after passing the distant blockade. Such spot-market transactions and rerouting are relatively common in global oil markets. Because the blockade would cause price spikes in China, international suppliers would have tremendous incentives to respond to this demand signal. Another challenge is that local states within the perimeter of the distant blockade might expand their trade ties in response to these incentives. These neutral states might reexport goods they acquired from foreign markets to China, which has been a long-standing problem for blockades throughout history.[16]

Short of patrolling the waters within the distant blockade's perimeter, the United States has several options to address rerouting and transshipment. One potential model is the British Navigational Certification (navicert) system from the First and Second World Wars.[17] Merchants would apply in advance for permission to pass the blockade, and U.S. authorities would investigate the risk of noncompliance. They would issue certificates to ships deemed to be low risk, and those certificates would ensure them safe passage. Ships without certification would be considered potential blockade-runners. Authorities could blacklist ships caught violating the embargo and impound them the next time they passed a choke point. To further enforce the blockade, the United States could apply economic pressure through secondary sanctions to get other countries to comply with an embargo on China, which would

---

[14] On the British experience in World War I, see Nicholas A. Lambert, *Planning Armageddon: British Economic Warfare and the First World War*, Cambridge, Mass.: Harvard University Press, 2012.

[15] For an overview of these challenges, see Collins and Murray, 2008.

[16] Gholz and Press, 2001; Mariya Grinberg, "Wartime Commercial Policy and Trade Between Enemies," *International Security*, Vol. 46, No. 1, Summer 2021.

[17] Collins, 2018, pp. 56–57.

also reduce the number of ships transiting the choke points.[18] However, this could increase international perceptions that the United States is acting too aggressively and thereby undermine international support for the embargo.

Chinese Countermeasures

China has been concerned for years that the United States might impose a blockade of key maritime choke points that would sever its access to international trade.[19] China has responded by developing partnerships with neighboring countries for overland pipeline construction—for example, with Russia, Kazakhstan, and Pakistan—and by increasing its strategic oil reserves, which now contain the equivalent of approximately 100 days of peacetime oil imports.[20] Additionally, China has prioritized port construction and access agreements in South Asia and the Indian Ocean region to develop alternative routes for oil imports through Indian Ocean ports with pipelines connecting them to western China.[21] On the military side, the PLA has upgraded its naval capabilities to conduct counterpiracy and SLOC protection missions, including augmenting shipboard missile defenses and ASW capabilities.[22]

Despite these actions, China remains vulnerable to disruption of imported oil supplies, and Chinese demand will likely continue to rise over the next decade.[23] China consumed around 14 million bpd in 2019 while producing less than 4 million bpd domestically.[24] During a conflict, China would likely ration domestic oil use, prioritizing supply for the PLA and essential industries and infrastructure. The combination of rationing supply, adding fuel extenders, and drawing on domestic production and strategic reserves would provide China with a considerable cushion against a distant blockade, particularly because disruption of

---

[18] Some states might be willing to sever their commercial ties with China because they share U.S. objectives. Others might be willing to do so only if the United States compensates them. The Allies did this in World War II with *preclusive purchasing*, which involved buying goods from neutral states to prevent Germany from acquiring them (David Baldwin, *Economic Statecraft*, Princeton, N.J.: Princeton University Press, 1985).

[19] Hu Jintao warned as early as 2003 about a "Malacca Dilemma" and ordered the PLA Navy to develop options to protect China's maritime interests (Cunningham, 2020, pp. 760–761).

[20] Aaron Clark and Sharon Cho, "China's Oil Reserves Are Close to Reaching Storage Capacity," Bloomberg, last updated February 26, 2021; Rosemary Kelanic, *Black Gold and Blackmail: Oil and Great Power Politics*, Ithaca, N.Y.: Cornell University Press, 2020, p. 179.

[21] Becker, 2020.

[22] Gunness, 2020.

[23] Taplin, 2021.

[24] N. Sönnichsen, "Oil Consumption in China from 1998 to 2019," Statista, January 5, 2021a; N. Sönnichsen, "Oil Production in China from 1998 to 2019," Statista, January 5, 2021b.

overseas trade would presumably reduce the energy demands of industry producing goods for export.[25]

China's access to overland imports would further blunt the blockade's economic impact. Russia is currently China's second largest oil supplier, and Russia and Kazakhstan together produce enough oil to meet China's requirements, although the infrastructure does not yet exist for these countries to divert all their oil exports to China.[26] However, China could also surge its import capacity by relying more on deliveries using highways and rail lines, which are inefficient but viable alternatives to pipelines.[27] Russia also ships around 600,000 bpd to China from the port of Kozmino in the Far East, which provides maritime supplies that do not transit choke points in Southeast Asia.[28] In short, while a distant blockade would place some pressure on China's economy, inflicting serious damage would take many months given that China would still have access to some oil imports and its strategic petroleum reserve. In theory, the United States could address this issue by attacking pipelines and related infrastructure targets in or near China, but conducting such strikes would fit poorly with the precepts of restraint.

To undermine a distant blockade, China could employ several measures that would increase the challenges for the United States in terms of response to China's actions and sustainment of the blockade. For example, China could send additional tankers to run the blockade. Borrowing from Iraq's responses to UN sanctions during and after the Gulf War, China could order many ships to run the blockade at the same time to overwhelm limited U.S. interdiction capacity, ignore U.S. Navy queries, cover ship decks with wire and oil, weld compartments shut, and disable vessels so that U.S. crews could not easily take control and redirect them to neutral ports.[29] China could also deploy paramilitary or special forces teams to violently resist U.S. boarding operations, which would consume time and attrit the specialized teams required for these missions, as well as create poor publicity and potentially undermine

---

[25] Collins, 2018, p. 59. Under conservative assumptions, China could retain access to oil supplies to sustain its military operations for at least ten months. This assumes that the PLA consumes no more than the U.S. military did at the peak of the war on terror, which included training and global peacetime deployments, and that China adds fuel extenders to oil from domestic production, strategic reserves, and overland imports (Collins, 2018, p. 67).

[26] Erickson and Collins, 2010, pp. 93–94. Russia recently expanded its pipeline capacity to 600,000 bpd, which currently covers around 6 percent of China's total oil imports. The pipeline from Kazakhstan has a capacity of 200,000 bpd.

[27] On the one hand, rail is only "slightly costlier" than pipelines, and suppliers regularly use it when demand exceeds pipeline capacity (Kelanic, 2020, pp. 179–190). On the other hand, Russia would have to balance the short-term price increases in Chinese markets with the costs of building new infrastructure and with the risk of disrupting its long-term export relationship with stable European markets (Glab, 2013).

[28] Olga Yagova, "As Russia Expands Pacific Pipeline, a Third of Oil Exports Go East," Reuters, November 21, 2019. China is also interested in further diversifying its shipping options through the Northern Sea Route to take advantage of efforts to develop Russian energy infrastructure in the Arctic.

[29] Cunningham, 2020, p. 750.

international support for the blockade, since China would circulate images of U.S. forces attacking ostensibly civilian crews.[30]

China could also use neutral-flagged vessels to run the blockade. It could provide lucrative rewards to neutral-flagged merchants and support them with forged documents, weapons, or paramilitary operatives. There is precedent for this technique. For example, North Korea has used vessels with flags of convenience that are registered to offshore holding companies and often fail to disclose port visits to circumvent international inspections.[31] China could also exploit normal business practices of purchasing oil on spot markets once tankers pass the distant blockade, which neutral states would likely assert is their right under international law. Third parties could deploy their own paramilitary units or naval escorts to deter U.S. interdiction under the pretext of resisting illegal operations to interfere with neutral trade on the high seas. It is not difficult, for example, to imagine Russia carrying out such operations with their oil tankers both to protect their profits and to undermine the United States politically. The United States conducted just such operations to defend its own neutral-flagged merchant ships during both World Wars I and II.[32]

China would presumably use a combination of carrots and sticks to try to undermine regional support for the U.S. blockade and encourage neutral states to assert their right to trade with China. "Carrots" could include economic incentives, such as joint energy exploration agreements for regional states, such as the Philippines, Vietnam, or other regional U.S. allies and partners that might tacitly support U.S. actions to push back on China's aggression, as China has done in the South China Sea to sway countries in its favor on territorial disputes.[33] China could also use "sticks" to punish countries, including directing its paramilitary forces to coerce regional supporters of the United States, engaging in cyberattacks, and threatening kinetic action or postwar economic reprisals to send a message to other states that remaining neutral is safe and profitable.[34] In addition to covertly bribing foreign officials to overlook what is passing through their ports, China could leverage its ownership of regional ports to make it difficult for the United States to use those facilities to sustain

---

[30] Lind and Press, 2018.

[31] Robert Huish, "The Failure of Maritime Sanctions Enforcement Against North Korea," *Asia Policy*, No. 23, January 2017, p. 132. North Korea operates a "fleet of ghost ships that paint false names on their hulls, steal identification numbers from other vessels and execute their trades via ship-to-ship transfers at sea, to avoid prying eyes at ports" (Jeanne Whalen, "Kim Jong Un Has a Fleet of Ghost Ships Sneaking Around the High Seas to Beat Sanctions," *Washington Post*, April 24, 2019; see also Mercy A. Kuo, "North Korea's Oil Procurement Networks," *The Diplomat*, April 27, 2021).

[32] Benjamin O. Fordham, "Revisionism Reconsidered: Exports and American Intervention in World War I," *International Organization*, Vol. 61, No. 2, Spring 2007.

[33] For an overview of China's activities in the South China Sea, see Ronald O'Rourke, *U.S.-China Strategic Competition in South and East China Seas: Background and Issues for Congress*, Washington, D.C.: Congressional Research Service, updated March 18, 2021a.

[34] Montgomery, 2013, p. 621.

the blockading forces.[35] The U.S. reward-and-punishment system designed to prevent China from undermining international support for the blockade would therefore have to compete with Chinese economic, diplomatic, and military threats and inducements in turn.

Beyond these measures, China has some military capacity to challenge the blockade. However, the ability to break it outright likely remains out of China's reach because the PLAN does not have the supporting logistical and C4ISR infrastructure to sustain and protect a sizable forward-deployed naval force over a long period, which a distant blockade scenario would require.[36] More likely, the PLAN and China Coast Guard would provide escorts for merchant ships to exploit any U.S. reluctance to directly engage the PLA in combat due to escalation concerns. The United States has the military capabilities to sink escorts, but the force requirements to deal with convoys would be far larger than those needed to deal with unescorted merchant vessels as in the case of sanctions enforcement against Iraq. The PLA could also threaten U.S. ships by conducting submarine and bomber patrols that would compel U.S. task groups to devote greater resources to force protection and cause disruptions to their boarding and inspection operations. These patrols could also target U.S. resupply and replenishment ships to curtail efforts to sustain the naval forces at the choke points. The PLA could interfere with U.S. blockade operations in a variety of other ways, such as through counterspace attacks, electronic warfare, and cyberattacks that would degrade U.S. networks and make ISR and communications more difficult for the blockading forces.[37]

Finally, if the blockade began to severely damage China's economy, and particularly if the United States were already engaged in a conflict with the PLA over Japan, China could impose retaliatory costs on the United States that would be intended to defeat it in a contest of resolve and compel it to end the blockade. China could attack U.S. regional bases with missiles, mine allied ports, or conduct cyberattacks against critical infrastructure in the United States or against U.S. military facilities in the region.[38] The PLAN could harass U.S. merchant ships in other parts of the region to impose costs on the United States in a symmetrical fashion, although anything more than limited actions would likely require too many resources for the PLAN to sustain.

---

[35] For an overview of Chinese port ownership and planned port construction in the region, see Mercator Institute for China Studies, "Mapping the Belt and Road Initiative: This Is Where We Stand," June 7, 2018.

[36] Joel Wuthnow, "The PLA Beyond Borders," in Joel Wuthnow, Arthur S. Ding, Phillip C. Saunders, Andrew Scobell, and Andrew N. D. Yang, eds., *The PLA Beyond Borders: Chinese Military Operations in Regional and Global Context*, Washington, D.C.: National Defense University Press, 2021, pp. 1–4.

[37] Glab, 2013.

[38] Collins and Murray, 2008, pp. 83, 88.

Implications for U.S. Posture and Force Structure

The United States would need significant naval capabilities to impose such a blockade. Using the UN coalition's maritime interdiction operations in the Gulf War, Fiona Cunningham estimates that blockades require roughly four surface ships for every ten merchant ships, assuming that the blockading forces board and inspect potential blockade-runners rather than simply sinking them.[39] The Gulf War example that Cunningham uses involved some countermeasures by Iraqi merchant ships, such as delayed responses to the Multinational Interception Force's (MIF's) instructions, razor wire on decks, and sailing together in an attempt to overwhelm MIF forces.[40] However, there was no major military opposition to the blockade. Therefore, the ratio of surface ships to merchant ships would likely be higher if the adversary's naval and other forces opposed the blockade. Still, this Gulf War analogy offers a baseline for calculating force requirements. Given the number of merchant ships that normally transit the Malacca, Sunda, and Lombok Straits during peacetime, Cunningham judges that intercepting just 25 percent of those ships would require 32 U.S. surface ships.[41]

We used Cunningham's approach to calculate how these estimates would change depending on whether blockading forces differentiate between oil tankers and other merchant vessels and intercept only the former (Table 5.1).

The Iraq analogy suggests that the United States would need on the order of 40 surface vessels to implement a blockade against all peacetime oil and gas tankers. However, there are several reasons why this is only a baseline for thinking about the number of vessels that the United States would need for the kind of distant blockade that we discuss in this chapter. On the one hand, commercial maritime traffic rates in wartime would be lower than peacetime traffic rates. On the other hand, the United States might want to stop at least some merchant ships beyond those carrying oil and gas. The United States could choose to lighten its

TABLE 5.1

Estimates of U.S. Forces Required for a Militarily Unopposed Blockade of China

Target Type	U.S. Surface Ships
All merchant ships	115
Only oil and gas tankers	42
25 percent of oil and gas tankers	13

NOTE: Estimates are for intercepting and conducting VBSS operations against unescorted ships, assuming that the number of vessels is unchanged from peacetime traffic.

---

[39] Cunningham, 2020, p. 751, footnote 102. On the logistics footprint required, see Cunningham, 2020, p. 758, footnote 117.

[40] Cunningham, 2020, p. 750.

[41] Cunningham, 2020, p. 758.

burden by intercepting some of the tankers instead of all of them, but, because the effects on China of blocking even 100 percent of its maritime energy imports would take a long time to develop, it is difficult to picture a substantially less complete interruption of supply being a very useful coercive tool.

Moreover, as discussed in the previous section, Chinese efforts to defy the blockade could greatly increase U.S. force requirements compared with the MIF's operations in the Arabian Gulf. For this reason, the 40–50-ship estimate likely represents the low end of the range of possibilities that prudent planners should consider when estimating force requirements for a distant blockade. China would certainly challenge the blockade both by supporting blockade-runners and by using PLAN and PLAAF forces to escort convoys or conduct direct attacks on U.S. ships enforcing the blockade. In addition, the PLAN's growing expeditionary capabilities make it likely that, in the next decade, China could sustain at least limited naval forces to challenge the blockade and hold U.S. forces at risk, which would increase U.S. Navy requirements to account for attrition and force protection. The United States would therefore likely need substantially more ships to stop the same number of commercial vessels than it did when implementing the blockade against Iraq.

A blockade that required a force of some 40–50 surface combatants (supported by MPA, long-endurance UAVs, and resupply ships) would be within the current capacity of the U.S. Navy, whose surface fleet currently includes 113 surface combatants—24 cruisers, 68 destroyers, and 21 frigates—in addition to its amphibious warfare fleet and the U.S. Coast Guard's national security cutters.[42]

Assuming that most of these forces would not routinely be present in the region under a grand strategy of restraint, the United States would have to deploy naval and land-based air forces from Guam, Hawaii, Alaska, and the continental United States. We estimate that the time required for the deployment of U.S. naval forces to Asia from Hawaii is around two weeks (Chapter Three), although air support would arrive faster. Given the planning principle that for every ship on a distant station there are two or more undergoing maintenance, working up for deployment, or in transit to or from their home ports, sustaining the blockade over months or years would represent a considerable demand on the U.S. Navy's forces that would require at least a similarly sized navy to today's or even a larger one.[43]

The long-term nature of a blockade would give the United States the luxury of time to assemble the ships, aircraft, and personnel needed to conduct it, meaning that the United States would not need to deploy the forces in question at the outset of a conflict, although it would want to have in place the logistics infrastructure to sustain them once they arrived in

---

[42] There are also 13 squadrons of P-8A Poseidon maritime patrol aircraft and one squadron of MQ-4C Triton maritime surveillance UAVs (International Institute for Strategic Studies, "North America," *Military Balance*, Vol. 121, No. 1, 2021b, pp. 51–54) and 62 combat logistics and fleet support ships ("Naval Vessel Register: Fleet Size," webpage, last updated 2021; Bruce Held and Brad Martin, "An American Force Structure for the 21st Century," *War on the Rocks*, July 8, 2021).

[43] Congressional Budget Office, *Crew Rotation in the Navy: The Long-Term Effect on Forward Presence*, Washington, D.C., Pub. No. 2987, October 2007, p. 5.

the theater. The United States could reduce the number of ships required depending on how effectively it enlisted support for the blockade from oil exporters who could prevent ships from sailing. The possibility of allies, such as Australia, contributing modest numbers of additional ships and aircraft to the effort could also help.

The United States would also want other military forces and security arrangements with local partners and allies to support the surface ships imposing the blockade. It would need a place to send merchant vessels that it does interdict. For example, the United States sent ships it seized during the MIF campaign to ports in nearby Gulf states, and it would need a local partner in the Asia-Pacific—ideally the closest countries, such as Indonesia or Malaysia, but if necessary Australia—to accept seized ships, sell or impound their cargo, and repatriate the multinational crews. In establishing these arrangements, the United States would need to deal with the challenge that many countries would likely be wary of accepting this role because of the potential for Chinese economic or military retaliation.

The United States would also need access to regional ports. Maintaining a logistics hub in Singapore, in addition to those in the Marianas, would assist the United States in sustaining the blockade. This would again run into the challenge that Singapore would likely be reluctant to support a blockade that would significantly affect its trade through the Strait of Malacca or invite retaliation by China. The United States would also ideally obtain legal permission from Indonesia and Malaysia to operate in their territorial waters near key choke points. Additionally, the United States would need access to air bases for land-based aircraft conducting ISR patrols and defending the airspace around the blockading forces, such as in northern Australia or India's Andaman Islands in the Bay of Bengal if the United States failed to secure basing access to support the blockade in Southeast Asian countries (e.g., Indonesia). Allies and partners could also assist the United States with ISR to detect the movement of Chinese ships and military forces.

Prewar discussions with other countries about the conditions under which they would support sanctions, grant basing or port access, and coordinate militarily during a conflict, up to the point of even contributing their own forces, would help lay the groundwork for regional support for a blockade. However, the United States would still face uncertainty about which countries would provide such support at the outset of a conflict and continue to do so throughout a long blockade. Countries in the region would face two competing considerations. In the face of a Chinese attack on Japan, other countries in the region might be willing to assist in checking Chinese aggression. At the same time, some countries might worry about Chinese military and economic retaliation. Having multiple potential partners could help the United States hedge against the loss of any one. Although Australia is more distant and therefore a less convenient location for supporting a blockade, its distance from China also makes it less vulnerable to Chinese military retaliation than other countries (although economic retaliation would remain possible). Therefore, the U.S.-Australian relationship is an especially important one to cultivate.

Conclusion

Using a distant blockade of key imports as a coercive instrument in a conflict with China is consistent with key precepts in most grand strategies of restraint. It would exploit the comparative advantages of the U.S. armed forces in the maritime commons, represent a way to use military power against China outside the reach of most of its A2/AD capabilities, and avoid directly striking China itself, which would limit U.S. losses and some, though not all, of the attendant escalatory pressures. Because its effects would accumulate gradually, taking time to move naval forces into the region to impose the blockade would not severely undermine its effectiveness (although doing so might affect its timeliness as a response). As a result, the blockade would not depend on having permanent U.S. naval forces stationed in the region, which would fit restrainers' inclinations to pull forces back from Asia.

Posture challenges would nevertheless remain. Unless the United States had great success convincing exporters to embargo trade with China, interdicting the vessels in question would require a sizable force of surface combatants and support vessels that a dramatically downsized U.S. Navy would have trouble providing. Having the cooperation of some states in the vicinity of principal sea-lanes and choke points would be important to sustaining the blockade effort, including access to local ports and military facilities. Such support, though, would likely become more challenging to enlist if the United States completely ended its forward presence and security commitments to the region under certain variants of restraint. At the very least, the United States would want to maintain strong security connections with relevant states in peacetime, even if it did not necessarily institutionalize those ties deeply, in order to retain the option to establish a viable blockade during a conflict. If the United States did not have support from local security partners, the requirements for the operation would be significantly greater, and it would require the United States to expand its logistical capabilities for continuous at-sea operations if it could not use regional ports to sustain the blockading forces.

The most likely application for a blockade under a grand strategy of restraint would be to contribute to the defense of Japan. Blockades are ill suited for quickly unfolding scenarios because of their slow-moving form of cost imposition, but, if the United States could help Japan hold out against a Chinese attack for some time, a blockade might be a useful supplement to build pressure for China to end the conflict. How much a blockade of China would add to the escalatory pressures that would already accompany U.S. military intervention in defense of Japan would depend on the nature and extent of the other U.S. actions against China. It would also depend on how severe the effects of the blockade were, including whether the United States confined itself to interdicting shipping or also mounted attacks on pipelines and other critical economic infrastructure to seriously disrupt overland supply to China from Russia, Central Asia, and South Asia. Ultimately, it is unclear before the fact whether a blockade would be so effective in imposing economic pain that it would help coerce China into backing down but not so coercive that it would prompt Chinese retaliation and escalation. Embracing a blockade as a policy option against China entails at least some degree of acceptance of such risk.

CHAPTER SIX

Conclusion

Findings

Many of our findings about the implications of strategies of restraint for U.S. posture are based on a preliminary analysis of three warfighting scenarios. As we discuss in the next section, analysts should conduct more-detailed analysis of these and other scenarios in the future to validate and refine these conclusions.

Restrainers Have a Variety of Views About When to Use Force in the Asia-Pacific

There is no single "grand strategy of restraint." Advocates of restraint generally agree that defending direct threats to the homeland should be the nation's top priority (as do most adherents to strategies that are more militarily assertive). Beyond this, the restraint community includes strategists with a variety of views about the threats that the United States faces and requirements for U.S. security. These divergent views lead to different prescriptions about when the United States should use force in the Asia-Pacific. Some restrainers believe that if China could direct the foreign policy of other powerful states in its region, such as Japan, or gain unimpeded access to the open ocean, it would seriously threaten U.S. security. These restrainers, therefore, would sustain the forces needed, forward if necessary, to assist with Japan's defense. But there are other restrainers who believe that the United States would remain secure even if China were able to dominate its neighbors, or who believe that it is unrealistic to imagine that China could achieve such dominance. As a result, these strategists are not inclined to use force to defend Japan (or other countries in the region) and would focus their military planning on protecting a more limited set of security interests closer to home. Therefore, the military posture implications ultimately depend on the variant of restraint in question.

For Many Restrainers, the Primary Driver of U.S. Posture in the Asia-Pacific Would Be the Defense of Japan

Defensive restrainers do not currently see any military objectives that require a substantial forward presence. However, flexible and counterhegemonic restrainers agree that the defense of Japan should be the highest-priority U.S. regional military objective (beyond the defense of the United States itself) because of Japan's strategic location and its economic and military strength. They want Japan to remain an independent power so that it can act as a counterweight to Chinese power and influence in the region. They also prefer that Japan maintain control of the Ryukyu Islands and surrounding waterways so that it could monitor and disrupt Chinese access to the open oceans. Some restrainers are, therefore, open to maintaining some level of forward presence to support this objective.

Defending Japan Against a Major Chinese Attack Would Likely Require Maintaining Some Forward-Deployed U.S. Naval Forces

To defend against a sudden, large-scale Chinese attack on the Japanese main islands and JSDF, the United States would likely need to have some forward-deployed naval forces in the region. Our preliminary analysis of a scenario involving a major Chinese attack on Japan's military and economy (Chapter Three) does not allow us to say with certainty how Japan's military would fare on its own in a major conflict with China. However, we know that China has a larger navy than Japan, and it is increasingly gaining ground in the qualitative competition. China is also making investments in airpower that could challenge Japan's air defenses and investments in offensive cyber capabilities that could target Japan's military command and control and critical infrastructure. Together, this suggests that Japan's military could face substantial losses relatively quickly in a major confrontation with China if current trends continue. Even if Japan significantly increased its defense spending in the next decade, it could not easily close its capability gap with China. Japan faces not only political and budgetary constraints but also demographic constraints on its ability to recruit potential military personnel. It also faces a dynamic competitor in China, which could respond by increasing its own military investments to stay ahead. Deploying naval forces from the continental United States would likely take two to three weeks (Chapter Three). Continuing to maintain at least some U.S. naval forces in the region (based in Guam or Japan or at sea in the Western Pacific Ocean) would hedge against the risk of large-scale attrition of the JSDF and provide more time for other U.S. forces to arrive.

Restrainers with concerns about the defense of Japan would also likely find the peacetime effects of such forces acceptable. Advocates of restraint generally prefer offshore naval forces to onshore ground forces or air forces, which they believe are particularly prone to disincentivize allies from burden-sharing because they appear to constitute an unambiguous commitment to the allies' defense. Restrainers would also consider how this presence would affect Chinese perceptions and behavior. Because having a peacetime naval posture in the region would likely reduce China's belief that it could successfully launch a rapid disarming attack on Japan, some restrainers would likely see this posture as enhancing extended deterrence if it did not discourage additional Japanese defense investment or appear to China to pose a serious offensive threat.

At least one of our scenarios envisions the need for rapid deployment of U.S. forces for the defense of Japan (Chapter Three). Pre-positioned equipment and materiel would enable U.S.

forces to be ready to operate more quickly given limited airlift and sealift capabilities. Moreover, all the scenarios for the defense of Japan in this report involve prolonged conflicts with China. Fighting longer conflicts requires supporting logistics and sustainment infrastructure that can supply and replenish forces over time. At a minimum, the United States would likely need to keep the facilities in Guam and Japan to pre-position materiel and stockpile munitions. The United States would not need to maintain facilities in South Korea for pre-positioned materiel for the scenarios discussed in this report. However, these could be important for restraint strategies that call for the defense of South Korea in a war against North Korea.

Restrainers Would Need to Prioritize Strategic Airlift and Sealift to Deploy Forces from the United States and for Survivability

The United States would likely have a smaller force in Japan under a grand strategy of restraint, so it would need to deploy an even larger proportion of the U.S. forces involved in a major conflict from the continental United States, Alaska, Hawaii, or potentially Australia, which are farther from key operating locations than many forward-deployed forces are in the current U.S. posture. It would need substantial airlift and sealift to deploy forces from these more distant locations. One trade-off that restraint would create, then, is having to expand the U.S. lift capacity to reduce U.S. permanent forward presence.

In addition, airlift and sealift are an important part of survivability in any conflict with China. China's large arsenal of missiles and its other capabilities, such as aircraft, pose a threat to U.S. forces at forward operating locations throughout the Asia-Pacific. The U.S. military envisions protecting U.S. air forces with a portfolio of responses, including spreading out aircraft to a larger number of operating locations, dispersing aircraft on each base, operating some from more-distant air bases, and hardening. Operating from more-distant locations requires air refueling capabilities, and basing architectures with dispersed operations or units likewise rely on airlift to move personnel, equipment, and supplies among air bases. Similarly, the United States might want to establish access to a greater number of ports to enhance the survivability of its naval forces, and it might want to strengthen the U.S. Navy's underway replenishment capabilities, such as oilers and other sealift assets, so that it can operate for longer periods at sea.

Restrainers' Limited Objectives in the Asia-Pacific Would Be Consistent with Reductions in Forward-Deployed Ground Forces and, Possibly, Land-Based Air Forces

Restrainers have consistently called for deploying fewer land-based air and ground forces abroad in peacetime. Our analysis suggests that this would be viable given the military missions that restrainers would prioritize. After considering restrainers' objectives and preferences for how to fight, we do not expect that the United States would deploy these forces in large numbers to defend Japan.[1]

Under variants of restraint that prioritize the defense of Japan, land-based air forces would have a central wartime role. However, our preliminary analysis suggests that these forces would not necessarily have to be present in peacetime, since the United States can deploy them quickly at the outset of a conflict, assuming that the United States and Japan maintain key facilities and that the U.S. military keeps the forces at a high readiness level and invests in relevant mobility capabilities, such as airlift and air-to-air refueling. That said, the United States does not currently have a large ground-based air presence in Japan relative to likely wartime needs,[2] and Japan subsidizes the cost of maintaining this presence. The United States and Japan would also need to regularly exercise joint air capabilities to ensure readiness for a conflict scenario, and there is uncertainty about how well Japan could defend its own airspace if it lacked U.S. support entirely at the outset of a conflict. Some advocates of restraint might, therefore, prefer to sustain the U.S. land-based air presence, or at least would not prioritize its reduction compared with other forces in the region. However, other restrainers might believe that a permanent presence could reduce Japan's incentives to invest in JASDF capabilities, so they might prefer to end the permanent presence of U.S. land-based air forces in Japan despite the military disadvantages of doing so.

There would be a limited wartime role and small peacetime presence for ground forces under a grand strategy of restraint. The United States could still station some U.S. Army forces in Japan during peacetime to manage facilities and pre-positioned stocks located there.[3] Army forces would deploy in larger numbers in wartime to provide key functions, such as air and base defense, logistics, and maintenance. Should the United States implement a blockade of China (Chapter Five), marines and soldiers could have a role in VBSS operations. These forces would not have to be present in the theater at the outbreak of conflict.

Restrainers are unlikely to support concepts that the U.S. Army and Marine Corps have been developing for a conflict with China that involve deploying relatively small units equipped with ground-based anti-ship, land-attack, or air defense missiles to attack the PLA from various forward locations.[4] Because these forces could not deploy quickly in wartime,

---

[1] We have not focused on North Korea contingencies in this report. For restraint grand strategies that call for defending South Korea against an attack from the North, there would likely be a somewhat larger role for ground forces in the Asia-Pacific.

[2] U.S. fixed-wing combat aircraft in Japan (including Okinawa) currently consist of two U.S. Air Force fighter wings (four squadrons), two squadrons of Marine Corps F-35Bs, detachments of Navy MPAs, and the air wing of the Japan-based carrier strike group when it is not at sea. Navy and Marine Corps fighter squadrons are approximately half as large (typically ten to 12 aircraft) as Air Force squadrons (International Institute for Strategic Studies, 2021b, p. 61).

[3] For example, U.S. Army forces currently maintain pre-positioned materiel and operate port facilities (U.S. Forces, Japan, undated).

[4] Terrence K. Kelly, Anthony Atler, Todd Nichols, and Lloyd Thrall, *Employing Land-Based Anti-Ship Missiles in the Western Pacific*, Santa Monica, Calif.: RAND Corporation, TR-1321-A, 2013; Mallory

they would have to be present in the region in peacetime or deployed during a crisis, which most restrainers would seek to avoid. Moreover, restrainers would likely argue that coastal defense missile forces and air defenses can and should belong to the countries that are protecting their own territory rather than be provided by the United States.

In addition to wartime military requirements, peacetime missions, such as security cooperation that strengthens interoperability and partners' military capacity, currently shape U.S. posture in the Asia-Pacific.[5] While restrainers are clear that they want allied states to have the capacity to defend themselves, they are less explicit about how the United States should approach security cooperation activities and how forward presence contributes to this mission.[6] Many flexible and counterhegemonic restrainers would still prioritize joint military exercises with Japan, but U.S. forces could temporarily rotate in from outside the region to participate in these events. Beyond the case of Japan, it is unclear how restrainers would approach security assistance for countries, such as the Philippines, that they generally prefer would remain independent but do not value enough to warrant direct military intervention. Given restrainers' general preference for a smaller peacetime forward presence, we assume that they would want to rely on rotational rather than permanent deployments for exercises and capacity-building. The United States already follows this model in its security relationship with the Philippines, so this would not represent a dramatic change.

Finally, restrainers do not generally support peacetime presence purely for the purpose of signaling U.S. willingness to defend another country. They would prioritize such a presence only in cases in which U.S. forces are needed to deny the adversary a quick victory that could harm U.S. interests, such as a major Chinese attack on Japan (Chapter Three).

Given China's Ability to Target Bases and Ports, the United States Would Still Need Access to a Large Number of Wartime Operating Locations in Partner Countries for Survivability

In addition to basing locations in Japan and Guam, restrainers have indicated a greater willingness to sustain U.S. defense relations with Australia. Because Australia has often contributed to U.S.-led operations, analysts often see it as an ally that appropriately shares the burden. It also enjoys the benefit of being located in the Asia-Pacific while being farther from China than are Japan, Taiwan, and South Korea. Restrainers might, therefore, want to engage in diplomacy to lay the groundwork for U.S. wartime access to Australian ports and airfields. Although Australia is unattractive as a location for U.S. fighter aircraft because of its distance from Japan, bombers operating from Australia could contribute to the defense of the

---

Shelbourne, "Marine Corps Ready to Conduct EABO Experiments with Allies in Indo-Pacific," *USNI News*, April 20, 2021.

[5] Consolidated Public Affairs Office, *III Marine Expeditionary Force and Marine Corps Installations Pacific: A Force in Readiness*, Marine Corps Base Camp S.D. Butler, Okinawa, Japan: III Marine Expeditionary Force and Marine Corps Installations Pacific, July 2012.

[6] Priebe et al., 2021, pp. 45, 78–81.

Ryukyus and U.S. Navy surface ships and submarines with access to Australian ports could similarly contribute to a blockade scenario. Yap and Palau could be attractive locations given the existing U.S. defense relationships and the potential to base naval and air forces farther away from China but still within reasonable distance to the region. This could further reduce U.S. dependence on Guam for distributed basing.

Having the Capability to Impose a Distant Blockade on China Would Require Maintaining a Large Navy and Having Wartime Access to Ports in the Region

In the scenario involving a U.S. blockade of China, we envisioned a diplomatic campaign for sanctions against China and VBSS operations at distant choke points targeting Chinese oil imports. Even assuming that many countries would voluntarily embargo energy exports to China and that the United States would focus on oil and gas tankers while allowing many other ships to pass without inspection, the United States would need a naval force of about the size of its current fleet to sustain such a blockade over time. If China contested the blockade with paramilitary and military forces, or if the United States needed to devote some naval forces to additional operations in a conflict scenario (such as defending the Ryukyus), the force requirements would be significantly more demanding. However, this force would not necessarily have to be as ready as the force currently is or be deployed forward in peacetime, since China would feel the effects of a blockade gradually regardless of how quickly the United States imposed it after a conflict started. If the United States could count on the active participation of a few key partner navies or widespread international compliance with the sanctions regime, the requirements for the size of the U.S. force could be smaller.

If the United States were to carry out the blockade without access to regional ports, it would require a larger logistical support force, such as oilers and combat logistics ships, to support continuous at-sea operations. The United States would therefore realistically need access to ports as sources of suppliers and repair and as locations for taking suspicious vessels that require further processing. It is difficult to know in advance which countries would be willing to provide access and sustain it over the course of a conflict in the face of Chinese retaliation and given the economic costs of wartime disruptions to trade with China. Because the United States would shift to a lower peacetime presence and narrower commitments in the region under a grand strategy of restraint, this could lead to new political alignments and calculations by traditional allies and partners that might reduce their willingness to support a costly blockade.

Like Current Policymakers, Restrainers Would Face Trade-Offs Between Maximizing U.S. Preparedness for Conflict and Incentivizing Burden-Sharing by Other States

Advocates of restraint generally call for U.S. retrenchment to encourage allies to do more for their own defense. However, to be well prepared to defend Japan, the United States would find it beneficial to take such steps as peacetime exercises and contingency planning with allies. The United States and Japan would want to maintain a level of interoperability between their armed forces to ensure that the two militaries can work together in a conflict. This would require regular military exercises with Japan's naval forces on such capabilities as ASW, as well as exercises with the JASDF, given that the United States would support Japan's air defenses in a conflict. The United States and Japan might also conduct exercises to enhance cybersecurity and resiliency of communications networks. In addition to conducting exercises, the U.S. military and the JASDF would want to ensure that both sides understand the protocols and procedures for coordinating operations during a conflict, particularly if the United States were to remove a significant portion of its permanent presence in Japan and would, therefore, be surging new deployments to Japan amid the chaos of a war.

Such policies would be at loggerheads with creating uncertainty about U.S. defense commitments to provoke allies to do more to defend themselves. That is, the same measures that the United States would want to undertake to maximize its preparedness for a war to defend Japan would signal to Japan that it can rely on the United States to guarantee its security. Counterhegemonic restrainers, who see the defense of Japan as a significant priority, might respond to this trade-off by erring on the side of military effectiveness over incentivizing burden-sharing. Flexible restrainers, who see the defense of Japan (or any other ally) as a lower priority, might be more willing to take risks in military effectiveness to reduce the risk that an ally will underinvest in its own defense.

Recommendations for Additional Analysis

This analysis provides a first-cut assessment of what U.S. force posture in the Asia-Pacific would look like under a grand strategy of restraint. It provides a framework for translating the relatively abstract theoretical principles of restraint into more-concrete policy implications for military planning. However, more-intensive modeling, wargaming, and other analysis remain necessary to provide a complete sense of what capabilities, capacity, and access the U.S. military would need in these scenarios.

Assess Japan's Ability to Defend Its Coasts and Airspace Against a Major Chinese Attack Without U.S. Support

Our preliminary analysis relies on information on trends in the quality and quantity of Chinese and Japanese military capabilities to assess where U.S. forces might be needed to supplement Japan's capabilities. To assess the military implications of restraint with greater fidelity, more-detailed analysis is needed. In particular, analysts should assess how Japan's armed forces would fare on their own in a conflict against China, with a focus on the defense of Japan's airspace and coasts. This is not because all restrainers expect Japan to fight on its own in the next decade. Rather, a better understanding of where Japan lacks capability or capacity, and how quickly those gaps would become serious problems in a conflict, would enable analysts to identify what forces and on what deployment timeline the United States would need to contribute to defend Japan effectively.

Such analysis should consider a variety of assumptions about the trajectory of expansion of the JSDF. Advocates of restraint expect that Japan will spend more on its own defense if the United States adopts a grand strategy of restraint, but there is uncertainty about exactly how domestic support for investment in the JSDF would change and how rapidly Japan could expand its forces. Evaluating the effects of these assumptions could help restrainers assess the level of risk that the United States would take on with different options for U.S. forward military posture.

Calculate Force and Logistics Requirements and Timelines for Deploying U.S. Air and Maritime Forces to Assess Which Forces Could Usefully Be Based Outside Japan

We use historical analogues to make rough predictions about how long it would take U.S. air and maritime forces to deploy to and within the Asia-Pacific. Future analysis should assess these timelines in more detail and consider how well these estimates hold in the context and at the level of conflict detailed in the specific scenarios in this report. This analysis might also consider how deployment timelines depend on different assumptions about readiness and basing within the United States, as well as logistics requirements for forces deploying to the region. There might be limiting factors, such as capacity for air-to-air refueling, that would determine capabilities that restrainers might wish to maintain or expand to ensure that U.S. deployments are fast and large enough to meet U.S. objectives with a smaller forward presence and that the United States has enough logistics capacity to sustain U.S. forces once they arrive in the region.

Demands for deployment speed, and, consequently, for force readiness, depend heavily on expectations about how quickly threats to vital U.S. interests could materialize and how much operational or strategic warning the United States would have. There are vast differences among needing to deploy in days or weeks before an ally suffers severe losses (the current norm in typical U.S. defense planning), being able to wait months or more before intervening to see if the ally is actually at risk of being conquered (as the United States did in World Wars I and II), and having years of warning because the potential enemy is not yet strong enough to pose a truly dangerous threat to U.S. national security (as Britain's interwar Ten-Year Rule illustrates).

Evaluate the Implications of Emerging Technologies for a Restraint-Oriented Posture in the Asia-Pacific

Like the vast majority of restraint scholarship, this report has focused on current and programmed rather than emerging technologies. However, technological advances may change the regional balance of power and the way that the United States, Japan, and China would fight. Future analysis should consider how such technologies—including advances in missile and missile defense, artificial intelligence, space and cyber, and electronic warfare capabilities—could affect the threats to restrainers' objectives, how the United States and countries in the region might fight in the event of war, and, ultimately, the implications for a restraint-oriented U.S. posture in the region.

Closing Thoughts

Theorists and advocates of restraint have much to say about the wars they think that the United States should not fight. This is one of the key differences that separates their prescriptions from those of traditional U.S. grand strategy. However, military posture—including force structure, where those forces are based, and what levels of readiness they maintain—is most fundamentally a function of what a nation's military forces must be able to accomplish. And identifying the key interests that the United States should be willing to risk war to defend is essential to understanding what alliances and other security commitments the United States should maintain, establish, or eliminate.

The scenarios presented in this report are intended to advance the discussion of what U.S. military posture should look like under a grand strategy of restraint. There will, of course, be some restrainers who are not interested in fighting or preparing to fight any of the wars in these scenarios, either because the stakes, risks, and prospects for success do not appear to add up to a worthwhile incentive for intervening or because the threat does not seem to be plausible enough to merit planning against. If so, the question that follows is what scenarios would meet the bar for guiding their military and regional security posture choices in the Asia-Pacific.

Abbreviations

A2/AD	anti-access/area denial
ASBM	anti-ship ballistic missile
ASCM	anti-ship cruise missile
ASW	anti-submarine warfare
bpd	barrels per day
C4ISR	command, control, communications, computers, intelligence, surveillance, and reconnaissance
DoD	U.S. Department of Defense
ICBM	intercontinental ballistic missile
IRBM	intermediate-range ballistic missile
ISR	intelligence, surveillance, and reconnaissance
JASDF	Japan Air Self-Defense Force
JMSDF	Japan Maritime Self-Defense Force
JSDF	Japan Self-Defense Forces
LACM	land-attack cruise missile
MIF	Multinational Interception Force
MPA	maritime patrol aircraft
MRBM	medium-range ballistic missile
PLA	People's Liberation Army
PLAAF	People's Liberation Army Air Force
PLAN	People's Liberation Army Navy
PLARF	People's Liberation Army Rocket Force
SAM	surface-to-air missile
SLBM	submarine-launched ballistic missile
SLOC	sea line of communication
SRBM	short-range ballistic missile
SSBN	nuclear-powered ballistic missile submarine
UAV	unmanned aerial vehicle
UN	United Nations
VBSS	visit, board, search, and seizure

References

III Marine Expeditionary Force, "III MEF Campaign Plan, 2015–2019," undated. As of October 25, 2021:
https://www.iiimef.marines.mil/Portals/22/Documents/III%20MEF%20Campaign%20Plan%20
Final%20(20140909)%20%20CG%20Approved.pdf?ver=2015-07-28-034630-773

Ashford, Emma, "Strategies of Restraint: Remaking America's Broken Foreign Policy," *Foreign Affairs*, Vol. 100, No. 5, September–October 2021, pp. 128–141.

Asia Maritime Transparency Initiative, "China Lands First Bomber on South China Sea Island," May 18, 2018.

Baldwin, David, *Economic Statecraft*, Princeton, N.J.: Princeton University Press, 1985.

Bandow, Doug, "It's Time for America to Cut South Korea Loose," *Foreign Policy*, April 13, 2017.

———, "Now's the Time to Become a Truly 'America First' Military," *American Conservative*, March 26, 2020.

Beauchamp-Mustafaga, Nathan, "Bomber Strike Packages with Chinese Characteristics," in Joel Wuthnow, Arthur S. Ding, Phillip C. Saunders, Andrew Scobell, and Andrew N. D. Yang, eds., *The PLA Beyond Borders: Chinese Military Operations in Regional and Global Context*, Washington, D.C.: National Defense University Press, 2021, pp. 199–234.

Becker, Jeffrey, *Securing China's Lifelines Across the Indian Ocean*, Newport, R.I.: China Maritime Studies Institute, U.S. Naval War College, China Maritime Report No. 11, December 2020.

Beckley, Michael, "The Emerging Military Balance in East Asia: How China's Neighbors Can Check Chinese Naval Expansion," *International Security*, Vol. 42, No. 2, 2017, pp. 78–119.

Bereiter, Gregory, *The U.S. Navy in Operation Enduring Freedom, 2001–2002*, Washington, D.C.: Naval History and Heritage Command, 2016.

Berteau, David J., Michael J. Green, Gregory T. Kiley, Nicholas F. Szechenyi, Ernest Z. Bower, Victor Cha, Karl F. Inderfurth, Christopher K. Johnson, Gary A. Powell, and Stephanie Sanok, *U.S. Force Posture Strategy in the Asia Pacific Region: An Independent Assessment*, Washington, D.C.: Center for Strategic and International Studies, 2012.

Biddle, Stephen, and Ivan Oelrich, "Future Warfare in the Western Pacific: Chinese Antiaccess/Area Denial, U.S. AirSea Battle, and Command of the Commons in East Asia," *International Security*, Vol. 41, No. 1, 2016, pp. 7–48.

"Biden Backs Trump Rejection of China's South China Sea Claim," *Politico*, July 11, 2021.

"Biden Wants Major Oil Reserve Sales. That's Not Easy in Asia," Bloomberg, last updated November 19, 2021.

Braumoeller, Bear F., "The Myth of American Isolationism," *Foreign Policy Analysis*, Vol. 6, No. 4, October 2010, pp. 349–371.

Brooks, Stephen G., "The Globalization of Production and the Changing Benefits of Conquest," *Journal of Conflict Resolution*, Vol. 43, No. 5, October 1999, pp. 646–670.

Brooks, Stephen G., G. John Ikenberry, and William C. Wohlforth, "Don't Come Home, America: The Case Against Retrenchment," *International Security*, Vol. 37, No. 3, Winter 2012–2013, pp. 7–51.

Brooks, Stephen G., and William C. Wohlforth, *America Abroad: Why the Sole Superpower Should Not Pull Back from the World*, New York: Oxford University Press, 2018.

Bureau of Economic Analysis, "Gross Domestic Product, (Third Estimate), GDP by Industry, and Corporate Profits, Fourth Quarter and Year 2020," news release, U.S. Department of Commerce, March 25, 2021.

Burke, Edmund J., Kristen Gunness, Cortez A. Cooper III, and Mark Cozad, *People's Liberation Army Operational Concepts*, Santa Monica, Calif.: RAND Corporation, RR-A394-1, 2020. As of October 6, 2021:
https://www.rand.org/pubs/research_reports/RRA394-1.html

Burke, Edmund J., Timothy R. Heath, Jeffrey W. Hornung, Logan Ma, Lyle J. Morris, and Michael S. Chase, *China's Military Activities in the East China Sea: Implications for Japan's Air Self-Defense Force*, Santa Monica, Calif.: RAND Corporation, RR-2574-AF, 2018. As of January 31, 2022:
https://www.rand.org/pubs/research_reports/RR2574.html

Burke, Matthew M., "Marines' Move from Okinawa to Guam Could Begin as Early as October 2024, Report Says," *Stars and Stripes*, May 16, 2019.

Byman, Daniel, and Matthew Waxman, *The Dynamics of Coercion: American Foreign Policy and the Limits of Military Might*, Cambridge, United Kingdom: Cambridge University Press, 2002.

Carpenter, Ted Galen, "Washington Needs to Jettison Its Commitment to Defend the Senkakus," Cato Institute, January 9, 2020.

Carpenter, Ted Galen, and Eric Gomez, "East Asia and a Strategy of Restraint," *War on the Rocks*, August 10, 2016.

Castillo, Jasen J., "Passing the Torch: Criteria for Implementing a Grand Strategy of Offshore Balancing," in Richard Fontaine and Loren DeJonge Schulman, eds., *New Voices in Grand Strategy*, Washington, D.C.: Center for a New American Security, 2019, pp. 23–35.

Center for Strategic and International Studies, "Significant Cyber Incidents Since 2006," incidents list, undated.

———, "How Much Trade Transits the South China Sea?" last updated January 25, 2021.

Central Intelligence Agency, "Japan," *World Factbook*, June 9, 2021. As of September 1, 2021:
https://www.cia.gov/the-world-factbook/countries/japan/#economy

Chang, Gordon C., "Now China Wants Okinawa, Site of U.S. Bases in Japan," *Daily Beast*, last updated June 26, 2017.

Chanlett-Avery, Emma, Caitlin Campbell, and Joshua A. Williams, *The U.S.-Japan Alliance*, Washington, D.C.: Congressional Research Service, RL33740, June 13, 2019.

Charles Koch Institute, "The Charles Koch Institute's Will Ruger on Status of U.S. Troop Withdrawal from Afghanistan," July 8, 2021.

Cheng, Dean, *Cyber Dragon: Inside China's Information Warfare and Cyber Operations*, Santa Barbara, Calif.: Praeger, 2016.

———, "Getting to Where the PLA Needs to Be," testimony presented before U.S.-China Economic and Security Review Commission, Washington, D.C., June 20, 2019.

Clark, Aaron, and Sharon Cho, "China's Oil Reserves Are Close to Reaching Storage Capacity," Bloomberg, last updated February 26, 2021.

Clark, Bryan, *The Emerging Era in Undersea Warfare*, Washington, D.C.: Center for Strategic and Budgetary Assessments, January 22, 2015.

Clark, Bryan, Timothy A. Walton, and Adam Lemon, *Strengthening the U.S. Defense Maritime Industrial Base: A Plan to Improve Maritime Industry's Contribution to National Security*, Washington, D.C.: Center for Strategic and Budgetary Assessments, 2020.

Colby, Elbridge, "Don't Let Iran Distract from China," *Wall Street Journal*, September 24, 2019.

———, *The Strategy of Denial: American Defense in an Age of Great Power Conflict*, New Haven, Conn.: Yale University Press, 2021.

Collins, Gabriel B., "A Maritime Oil Blockade Against China—Tactically Tempting but Strategically Flawed," *Naval War College Review*, Vol. 71, No. 2, Spring 2018, pp. 49–78.

Collins, Gabriel B., and William S. Murray, "No Oil for the Lamps of China?" *Naval War College Review*, Vol. 61, No. 2, Spring 2008, pp. 1–17.

Commander, Navy Installations Command, "Commander, Joint Region Marianas: Naval Base Guam," webpage, undated. As of October 4, 2021:
https://www.cnic.navy.mil/regions/jrm/installations/navbase_guam.html

Commander, Navy Region Hawaii, "Fleet Information," webpage, undated. As of June 16, 2021:
https://www.cnic.navy.mil/regions/cnrh/about/fleet_information.html

Commander, U.S. 7th Fleet, "The United States Seventh Fleet," webpage, undated. As of September 22, 2021:
https://www.c7f.navy.mil/About-Us/Facts-Sheet/

Congressional Budget Office, *Crew Rotation in the Navy: The Long-Term Effect on Forward Presence*, Washington, D.C., Pub. No. 2987, October 2007.

Consolidated Public Affairs Office, *III Marine Expeditionary Force and Marine Corps Installations Pacific: A Force in Readiness*, Marine Corps Base Camp S.D. Butler, Okinawa, Japan: III Marine Expeditionary Force and Marine Corps Installations Pacific, July 2012.

Costello, John, and Joe McReynolds, "China's Strategic Support Force: A Force for a New Era," in Phillip C. Saunders, Arthur S. Ding, Andrew Scobell, Andrew N. D. Yang, and Joel Wuthnow, eds., *Chairman Xi Remakes the PLA: Assessing Chinese Military Reforms*, Washington, D.C.: National Defense University Press, 2019, pp. 437–515.

Coté, Owen R., Jr., *Assessing the Undersea Balance Between the U.S. and China*, Cambridge, Mass.: MIT Security Studies Program, SSP Working Paper, 2011. As of September 21, 2021:
https://drive.google.com/file/d/0B_ph0c6i87C_X00wNXlVQVJMUWM/view?resourcekey=0-tLlP8uHq533x8S07-opj-g

Cropsey, Seth, Jun Isomura, and James Conway, *U.S.-Japan Cooperation on Strategic Island Defense*, Washington, D.C.: Hudson Institute, 2018.

Cunningham, Fiona S., "The Maritime Rung on the Escalation Ladder: Naval Blockades in a US-China Conflict," *Security Studies*, Vol. 29, No. 4, 2020, pp. 730–768.

———, "Testimony Before the U.S.-China Economic and Security Review Commission," hearing on "Deterring PRC Aggression Towards Taiwan," February 18, 2021, Washington, D.C.: U.S.-China Economic and Security Review Commission, 2021.

Defense Intelligence Agency, *China Military Power: Modernizing a Force to Fight and Win*, Washington, D.C., 2019.

Defense Intelligence Ballistic Missile Analysis Committee, *Ballistic and Cruise Missile Threat*, Wright-Patterson Air Force Base, Ohio: National Air and Space Intelligence Center, 2020.

Defense Security Cooperation Agency, "Japan—F-35 Joint Strike Fighter Aircraft," news release, Washington, D.C., July 9, 2020.

Deudney, Daniel, and G. John Ikenberry, "Misplaced Restraint: The Quincy Coalition Versus Liberal Internationalism," *Survival*, Vol. 63, No. 4, August–September 2021, pp. 7–32.

"Document: China's Military Strategy," USNI News, last updated May 26, 2015.

DoD—*See* U.S. Department of Defense.

Downes, Alexander B., and Jonathan Monten, "Does Spreading Democracy by Force Have a Place in US Grand Strategy? A Skeptical View," in A. Trevor Thrall and Benjamin H. Friedman, eds., *US Grand Strategy in the 21st Century: The Case for Restraint*, New York: Routledge, 2018, pp. 80–107.

Easton, Ian, *The Chinese Invasion Threat: Taiwan's Defense and American Strategy in Asia*, Arlington, Va.: Project 2049 Institute, 2017.

———, *China's Top Five War Plans*, Arlington, Va.: Project 2049 Institute, Policy Brief 19-001, 2019.

Erickson, Andrew, "China's DF-21D and DF-26B ASBMs: Is the U.S. Military Ready?" *RealClearDefense*, November 16, 2020.

Erickson, Andrew, and Gabriel B. Collins, "Beijing's Energy Security Strategy: The Significance of a Chinese State-Owned Tanker Fleet," *Orbis*, Vol. 51, No. 4, Fall 2007, pp. 665–684.

———, "China's Oil Security Pipe Dream—The Reality, and Strategic Consequences, of Seaborne Imports," *Naval War College Review*, Vol. 63, No. 2, Spring 2010, pp. 89–111.

Erickson, Andrew S., and Joel Wuthnow, "Barriers, Springboards and Benchmarks: China Conceptualizes the Pacific 'Island Chains,'" *China Quarterly*, Vol. 225, March 2016, pp. 1–22.

Fish, Tim, "Japan Maritime Self-Defense Force Expanding as Tokyo Takes New Approach to Maritime Security," USNI News, May 29, 2019.

Fordham, Benjamin O., "Revisionism Reconsidered: Exports and American Intervention in World War I," *International Organization*, Vol. 61, No. 2, Spring 2007, pp. 277–310.

Friedman, Benjamin H., *Bad Idea: Permanent Alliances*, Defense 360, Washington, D.C.: Center for Strategic and International Studies, December 2018.

———, *Restraint: A Post-COVID-19 U.S. National Security Strategy*, Washington, D.C.: Defense Priorities, 2020.

Friedman, Benjamin H., and Justin Logan, "Why the U.S. Military Budget Is 'Foolish and Sustainable,'" *Orbis*, Vol. 56, No. 2, Spring 2012, pp. 177–191.

Gady, Franz-Stefan, "China's Navy Deploys New H-6J Anti-Ship Cruise Missile-Carrying Bombers," *The Diplomat*, October 12, 2018.

Gartzke, Erik, "The Myth of Cyberwar: Bringing War in Cyberspace Back Down to Earth," *International Security*, Vol. 38, No. 2, Fall 2013, pp. 41–73.

Gavin, Francis J., "Strategies of Inhibition: U.S. Grand Strategy, the Nuclear Revolution, and Nonproliferation," *International Security*, Vol. 40, No. 1, Summer 2015, pp. 9–46.

Gerstenzang, James, "Willing to Blockade Iraq to Stop Any Oil Shipment, Bush Says: Sanctions: But the President Reports That the U.N. Embargo Has Virtually Halted World Trade with Baghdad," *Los Angeles Times*, August 12, 1990.

Gholz, Eugene, Benjamin H. Friedman, and Enea Gjoza, "Defensive Defense: A Better Way to Protect US Allies in Asia," *Washington Quarterly*, Vol. 42, No. 4, Winter 2020, pp. 171–189.

Gholz, Eugene, and Daryl G. Press, "The Effects of Wars on Neutral Countries: Why It Doesn't Pay to Preserve the Peace," *Security Studies*, Vol. 10, No. 4, Summer 2001, pp. 1–57.

Gholz, Eugene, Daryl G. Press, and Harvey M. Sapolsky, "Come Home, America: The Strategy of Restraint in the Face of Temptation," *International Security*, Vol. 21, No. 4, Spring 1997, pp. 5–48.

Girard, Bonnie, "China and Gulf Security: Conspicuous by Its Absence," *The Diplomat*, May 7, 2020.

Glab, Jason, "Blockading China: A Guide," *War on the Rocks*, October 1, 2013.

Glaser, Charles L., "A U.S.-China Grand Bargain? The Hard Choice Between Military Competition and Accommodation," *International Security*, Vol. 39, No. 4, Spring 2015, pp. 49–90.

Glaser, John, Christopher A. Preble, and A. Trevor Thrall, "Towards a More Prudent American Grand Strategy," *Survival*, Vol. 61, No. 5, 2019, pp. 25–42.

Gordon, Michael R., "Confrontation in the Gulf: Navy Begins Blockade Enforcing Iraq Embargo," *New York Times*, August 17, 1990.

Grabow, Colin, *Responsible Stakeholders: Why the United States Should Welcome China's Economic Leadership*, Washington, D.C.: Cato Institute, Policy Analysis No. 821, October 3, 2017.

Grady, John, "Russia Is Top Military Threat to U.S. Homeland, Air Force General Says," USNI News, August 18, 2021.

Gregson, Wallace C., Jr., and Jeffrey W. Hornung, "The United States Considers Reinforcing Its 'Pacific Sanctuary,'" *War on the Rocks*, April 12, 2021.

Grinberg, Mariya, "Wartime Commercial Policy and Trade Between Enemies," *International Security*, Vol. 46, No. 1, Summer 2021, pp. 9–52.

Grossman, Derek, "Biden's Indo-Pacific Policy Blueprint Emerges," Nikkei Asia, August 23, 2021.

Gunness, Kristen, "The China Dream and the Near Seas," in Roy Kamphausen, David Lai, and Tiffany Ma, eds., *Securing the China Dream: The PLA's Role in a Time of Reform and Change*, Seattle, Wash.: National Bureau of Asian Research, 2020, pp. 75–91.

———, "The PLA's Expeditionary Force: Current Capabilities and Trends," in Joel Wuthnow, Arthur S. Ding, Phillip C. Saunders, Andrew Scobell, and Andrew N. D. Yang, eds., *The PLA Beyond Borders: Chinese Military Operations in Regional and Global Context*, Washington, D.C.: National Defense University Press, 2021, pp. 23–49.

Hamilton, Thomas, and David Ochmanek, *Operating Low-Cost, Reusable Unmanned Aerial Vehicles in Contested Environments: Preliminary Evaluation of Operational Concepts*, Santa Monica, Calif.: RAND Corporation, RR-4407-AF, 2020. As of October 6, 2021: https://www.rand.org/pubs/research_reports/RR4407.html

Hammes, T. X., *Offshore Control: A Proposed Strategy for an Unlikely Conflict*, Washington, D.C.: Institute for National Strategic Studies, National Defense University, No. 278, June 2012.

Harold, Scott, Koichiro Bansho, Jeffrey W. Hornung, Koichi Isobe, and Richard L. Simcock II, *U.S.-Japan Alliance Conference: Meeting the Challenge of Amphibious Operations*, Santa Monica, Calif.: RAND Corporation, CF-387-GOJ, 2018. As of January 31, 2022:
https://www.rand.org/pubs/conf_proceedings/CF387.html

Hartman, Jim, "The United States and Japan Still Benefit from Complementary Maritime Capabilities," *War on the Rocks*, March 9, 2021.

Heath, Timothy R., "Chinese Political and Military Thinking Regarding Taiwan and the East and South China Seas," testimony presented before the U.S.-China Economic and Security Review Commission on April 13, 2017, Santa Monica, Calif.: RAND Corporation, CT-470, 2017. As of January 31, 2022:
https://www.rand.org/pubs/testimonies/CT470.html

Heerdt, William, "Russian Hard Power Projection: A Brief Synopsis," blog post, *Post-Soviet Post*, March 25, 2020.

Heginbotham, Eric, Michael Nixon, Forrest E. Morgan, Jacob L. Heim, Jeff Hagen, Sheng Li, Jeffrey Engstrom, Martin C. Libicki, Paul DeLuca, David A. Shlapak, David R. Frelinger, Burgess Laird, Kyle Brady, and Lyle J. Morris, *The U.S.-China Military Scorecard: Forces, Geography, and the Evolving Balance of Power, 1996–2017*, Santa Monica, Calif.: RAND Corporation, RR-392-AF, 2015. As of September 15, 2021:
https://www.rand.org/pubs/research_reports/RR392.html

Heginbotham, Eric, and Richard J. Samuels, "Active Denial: Redesigning Japan's Response to China's Military Challenge," *International Security*, Vol. 42, No. 4, Spring 2018, pp. 128–169.

Held, Bruce, and Brad Martin, "An American Force Structure for the 21st Century," *War on the Rocks*, July 8, 2021.

Hicks, Kathleen H., and Joseph P. Federici, *Getting to Less? Exploring the Press for Less in America's Defense Commitments*, Washington, D.C.: Center for Strategic and International Studies, CSIS Briefs, January 2020.

Holland, Steve, and Kiyoshi Takenaka, "Trump Says U.S. Committed to Japan Security, in Change from Campaign Rhetoric," Reuters, February 10, 2017.

Hornung, Jeffrey W., *Japan's Potential Contributions in an East China Sea Contingency*, Santa Monica, Calif.: RAND Corporation, RR-A314-1, 2020a. As of January 31, 2022:
https://www.rand.org/pubs/research_reports/RRA314-1.html

———, "Japan Is Canceling a U.S. Missile Defense System," *Foreign Policy*, July 2, 2020b. As of September 30, 2021:
https://foreignpolicy.com/2020/07/02/japan-aegis-ashore-expense-cancel-united-states-alliance/

Hornung, Jeffrey W., and Scott W. Harold, "Japan's Potential Acquisition of Ground-Launched Land-Attack Missiles: Implications for the U.S.-Japanese Alliance," *War on the Rocks*, September 9, 2021.

Hughes, Llewelyn, "Why Japan Will Not Go Nuclear (Yet): International and Domestic Constraints on the Nuclearization of Japan," *International Security*, Vol. 31, No. 4, Spring 2007, pp. 67–96.

Hughes, Llewelyn, and Austin Long, "Is There an Oil Weapon? Security Implications of Changes in the Structure of the International Oil Market," *International Security*, Vol. 39, No. 3, Winter 2014–2015, pp. 152–189.

Huish, Robert, "The Failure of Maritime Sanctions Enforcement Against North Korea," *Asia Policy*, No. 23, January 2017, pp. 131–152.

Hurst, Daniel, "Peter Dutton Flags More US Troops on Australian Soil Citing Potential China Conflict," *The Guardian*, June 10, 2021.

Iida, Masafumi, *China's Security Threats and Japan's Responses*, Washington, D.C.: Center for Strategic and International Studies, 2021.

International Institute for Strategic Studies, "Chapter Five: China's Cyber Power in a New Era," *Asia Pacific Regional Security Assessment 2019*, Washington, D.C., 2019, pp. 77–90.

———, "Asia," *Military Balance*, Vol. 121, No. 1, 2021a, pp. 218–313.

———, "North America," *Military Balance*, Vol. 121, No. 1, 2021b, pp. 30–65.

"Is U.S. Foreign Policy Too Hostile to China? *Foreign Affairs* Asks the Experts," *Foreign Affairs*, October 19, 2021.

Izumikawa, Yasuhiro, "Explaining Japanese Antimilitarism: Normative and Realist Constraints on Japan's Security Policy," *International Security*, Vol. 35, No. 2, Fall 2010, pp. 123–160.

Japan Ministry of Defense, *Defense of Japan 2020*, Tokyo, 2020a.

———, "Part III: Three Pillars of Japan's Defense," *Defense of Japan 2020*, Tokyo, 2020b. As of June 16, 2021:
https://www.mod.go.jp/en/publ/w_paper/wp2020/pdf/index.html

Japan Ministry of Foreign Affairs, "Senkaku Islands Q&A," webpage, April 13, 2016. As of September 23, 2021:
https://www.mofa.go.jp/region/asia-paci/senkaku/qa_1010.html

"Japan's Food Self-Sufficiency Rate Marks 38 Percent in Fiscal 2019, Far from Its Target of 45 Percent," *Japan Agricultural News*, August 11, 2020.

Katsoulas, Fotios, "Monthly Report: Japan's Crude Imports Soar to 2.9MMbpd in August," IHS Markit, August 18, 2021.

Kelanic, Rosemary, *Black Gold and Blackmail: Oil and Great Power Politics*, Ithaca, N.Y.: Cornell University Press, 2020.

Kelly, Terrence K., Anthony Atler, Todd Nichols, and Lloyd Thrall, *Employing Land-Based Anti-Ship Missiles in the Western Pacific*, Santa Monica, Calif.: RAND Corporation, TR-1321-A, 2013. As of February 1, 2022:
https://www.rand.org/pubs/technical_reports/TR1321.html

Kelly, Tim, "Japan to Develop Longer-Range Anti-Ship Missiles as China Pressure Mounts," Reuters, December 18, 2020.

Kelly, Tim, and Ju-min Park, "Analysis: With an Eye on China, Japan's Ruling Party Makes Unprecedented Defence Spending Pledge," Reuters, October 31, 2021.

Khalilzad, Zalmay, and David Ochmanek, "Rethinking US Defence Planning," *Survival*, Vol. 39, No. 1, Spring 1997, pp. 43–64.

Knoema, "Japan - Production of Crude Oil Including Lease Condensate," webpage, undated. As of December 3, 2021:
https://knoema.com/atlas/Japan/topics/Energy/Oil/Production-of-crude-oil

Kotani, Tetsuo, "China's Military and Paramilitary Activities in the East China Sea: Trends and Assessments for the U.S.-Japan Alliance," *Asia Policy*, Vol. 15, No. 3, July 2020, pp. 7–17.

Kristensen, Hans M., and Matt Korda, "Chinese Nuclear Forces, 2019," *Bulletin of the Atomic Scientists*, Vol. 75, No. 4, 2019, pp. 171–178.

Kristensen, Hans M., and Robert S. Norris, "United States Nuclear Forces, 2017," *Bulletin of the Atomic Scientists*, Vol. 73, No. 1, 2017, pp. 48–57.

Kumagai, Takeo, "Japan to Sell Part of National Oil Reserves by Advancing Crude Grade Replacement Plans," S&P Global, November 24, 2021.

Kuo, Mercy A., "North Korea's Oil Procurement Networks," *The Diplomat*, April 27, 2021.

Kupchan, Charles A., *Isolationism: A History of America's Efforts to Shield Itself from the World*, New York: Oxford University Press, 2020.

Lambert, Nicholas A., *Planning Armageddon: British Economic Warfare and the First World War*, Cambridge, Mass.: Harvard University Press, 2012.

Larson, Eric V., *Force Planning Scenarios, 1945–2016: Their Origins and Use in Defense Strategic Planning*, Santa Monica, Calif.: RAND Corporation, RR-2173/1-A, 2019. As of February 18, 2022:
https://www.rand.org/pubs/research_reports/RR2173z1.html

Larter, David B., "Surface Ship Readiness Continues to Struggle, US Navy Inspections Show," *Defense News*, March 3, 2021.

Layne, Christopher, "From Preponderance to Offshore Balancing: America's Future Grand Strategy," *International Security*, Vol. 22, No. 1, Summer 1997, pp. 86–124.

———, *The Peace of Illusions: American Grand Strategy from 1940 to the Present*, Ithaca, N.Y.: Cornell University Press, 2006.

———, "Coming Storms: The Return of Great-Power War," *Foreign Affairs*, Vol. 99, No. 6, November–December 2020, pp. 42–49.

Leary, Alex, and Bob Davis, "Biden's China Policy Is Emerging—And It Looks a Lot Like Trump's," *Wall Street Journal*, June 10, 2021.

Lendon, Brad, and Blake Essig, "Japan's Defense Minister Draws Red Line in Island Dispute with China," CNN, September 16, 2021.

Lewis, James Andrew, *U.S.-Japan Cooperation in Cybersecurity*, Washington, D.C.: Center for Strategic and International Studies, November 2015.

Liberman, Peter, *Does Conquest Pay? The Exploitation of Occupied Industrial Societies*, Princeton, N.J.: Princeton University Press, 1996.

Lin, Bonny, "U.S. Allied and Partner Support for Taiwan: Responses to a Chinese Attack on Taiwan and Potential U.S. Taiwan Policy Changes," testimony presented before the U.S.-China Economic and Security Review Commission on February 18, 2021, Santa Monica, Calif.: RAND Corporation, CT-A1194-1, 2021. As of September 24, 2021:
https://www.rand.org/pubs/testimonies/CTA1194-1.html

Lind, Jennifer, "Keep, Toss, or Fix? Assessing US Alliance in East Asia," in Jeremi Suri and Benjamin Valentino, eds., *Sustainable Security: Rethinking American National Security Strategy*, Oxford: Oxford University Press, 2016.

Lind, Jennifer, and Daryl G. Press, "Markets or Mercantilism? How China Secures Its Energy Supplies," *International Security*, Vol. 42, No. 4, Spring 2018, pp. 170–204.

Lingel, Sherrill, Jeff Hagen, Eric Hastings, Mary Lee, Matthew Sargent, Matthew Walsh, Li Ang Zhang, and David Blancett, *Joint All-Domain Command and Control for Modern Warfare: An Analytic Framework for Identifying and Developing Artificial Intelligence Applications*, Santa Monica, Calif.: RAND Corporation, RR-4408/1-AF, 2020. As of October 6, 2021:
https://www.rand.org/pubs/research_reports/RR4408z1.html

Lostumbo, Michael J., Michael J. McNerney, Eric Peltz, Derek Eaton, David R. Frelinger, Victoria A. Greenfield, John Halliday, Patrick Mills, Bruce R. Nardulli, Stacie L. Pettyjohn, Jerry M. Sollinger, and Stephen M. Worman, *Overseas Basing of U.S. Military Forces: An Assessment of Relative Costs and Strategic Benefits*, Santa Monica, Calif.: RAND Corporation, RR-201-OSD, 2013. As of February 11, 2022:
https://www.rand.org/pubs/research_reports/RR201.html

Luce, LeighAnn, and Erin Richter, "Handling Logistics in a Reformed PLA: The Long March Toward Jointness," in Phillip C. Saunders, Arthur S. Ding, Andrew Scobell, Andrew N. D. Yang, and Joel Wuthnow, eds., *Chairman Xi Remakes the PLA: Assessing Chinese Military Reforms*, Washington, D.C., National Defense University Press, 2019, pp. 257–292.

Marie, Kimberly, *United States Agricultural Exports to Japan Remain Promising*, Washington, D.C.: U.S. Department of Agriculture, International Agricultural Trade Report, June 5, 2018.

Marine Rotational Force, "U.S. Marines Complete Their Ninth Rotation in Australia," U.S. Indo-Pacific Command, October 22, 2020.

Mastro, Oriana Skylar, "Conflict and Chaos on the Korean Peninsula: Can China's Military Help Secure North Korea's Nuclear Weapons?" *International Security*, Vol. 43, No. 2, Fall 2018, pp. 84–116.

———, "The Taiwan Temptation: Why Beijing Might Resort to Force," *Foreign Affairs*, Vol. 100, No. 4, July–August 2021, pp. 58–67.

Mattis, Jim, *Summary of the 2018 National Defense Strategy of the United States of America*, Washington, D.C.: Department of Defense, 2018.

Mazarr, Michael J., Katharina Ley Best, Burgess Laird, Eric V. Larson, Michael E. Linick, and Dan Madden, *The U.S. Department of Defense's Planning Process: Components and Challenges*, Santa Monica, Calif.: RAND Corporation, RR-2173/2-A, 2019. As of February 1, 2022:
https://www.rand.org/pubs/research_reports/RR2173z2.html

Mazza, Michael, "Why Defending Taiwan Is an American Political Consensus," American Enterprise Institute, Global Taiwan Institute, November 4, 2020.

McCaslin, Ian Burns, and Andrew S. Erickson, "The Impact of Xi-Era Reforms on the Chinese Navy," in Phillip C. Saunders, Arthur S. Ding, Andrew Scobell, Andrew N. D. Yang, and Joel Wuthnow, eds., *Chairman Xi Remakes the PLA: Assessing Chinese Military Reforms*, Washington, D.C.: National Defense University Press, 2019, pp. 125–170.

McCurry, Justin, "China Lays Claim to Okinawa as Territory Dispute with Japan Escalates," *The Guardian*, May 15, 2013.

Mearsheimer, John J., *The Tragedy of Great Power Politics*, New York: W. W. Norton & Company, 2001.

———, *The Great Delusion: Liberal Dreams and International Realities*, New Haven, Conn.: Yale University Press, 2018.

Mearsheimer, John J., and Stephen M. Walt, "The Case for Offshore Balancing: A Superior U.S. Grand Strategy," *Foreign Affairs*, Vol. 95, No. 4, July–August 2016, pp. 70–83.

Mercator Institute for China Studies, "Mapping the Belt and Road Initiative: This Is Where We Stand," June 7, 2018.

Middlebrook, Martin, *The Falklands War, 1982*, New York: Penguin, 2001.

Miller, Nicholas L., *Stopping the Bomb: The Sources and Effectiveness of US Nonproliferation Policy*, Ithaca, N.Y.: Cornell University Press, 2018.

Mills, Patrick, Adam Grissom, Jennifer Kavanagh, Leila Mahnad, and Stephen M. Worman, *A Cost Analysis of the U.S. Air Force Overseas Posture: Informing Strategic Choices*, Santa Monica, Calif.: RAND Corporation, RR-150-AF, 2013. As of October 25, 2021:
https://www.rand.org/pubs/research_reports/RR150.html

Ministry of Foreign Affairs of Japan, *The Guidelines for Japan-U.S. Defense Cooperation*, Tokyo, April 27, 2015.

Mirski, Sean, "Stranglehold: The Context, Conduct and Consequences of an American Naval Blockade of China," *Journal of Strategic Studies*, Vol. 36, No. 3, 2013, pp. 385–421.

Montgomery, Evan Braden, *Defense Planning for the Long Haul: Scenarios, Operational Concepts, and the Future Security Environment*, Washington, D.C.: Center for Strategic and Budgetary Assessments, 2009.

———, "Reconsidering a Naval Blockade of China: A Response to Mirski," *Journal of Strategic Studies*, Vol. 36, No. 4, 2013, pp. 615–623.

Mueller, John, *The Stupidity of War: American Foreign Policy and the Case for Complacency*, Cambridge, United Kingdom: Cambridge University Press, 2021.

Mueller, Karl P., Jasen J. Castillo, Forrest E. Morgan, Negeen Pegahi, and Brian Rosen, *Striking First: Preemptive and Preventive Attack in U.S. National Security Policy*, Santa Monica, Calif.: RAND Corporation, MG-403-AF, 2006. As of September 10, 2021:
https://www.rand.org/pubs/monographs/MG403.html

National Geospatial-Intelligence Agency, *Pub. 151: Distances Between Ports*, 11th ed., Bethesda, Md., 2001.

National Security Council, "U.S. Strategic Framework for the Indo-Pacific," Washington, D.C., February 2018.

Naval Vessel Register, "Fleet Size," webpage, last updated 2021. As of September 7, 2021:
https://www.nvr.navy.mil/NVRSHIPS/FLEETSIZE.HTML

Nevitt, Mark, "The US-Philippines Defense Treaty and the Pompeo Doctrine on South China Sea," *Just Security*, March 11, 2019.

Newsham, Grant, and Benjamin Self, "Resolved: Japan Should Deepen Defense/Security Cooperation with Taiwan," *Debating Japan*, Vol. 3, No. 3, April 2, 2020.

O'Brien, Robert C., "A Free and Open Indo-Pacific," White House, January 5, 2021.

Ochmanek, David, Peter A. Wilson, Brenna Allen, John Speed Meyers, and Carter C. Price, *U.S. Military Capabilities and Forces for a Dangerous World: Rethinking the U.S. Approach to Force Planning*, Santa Monica, Calif.: RAND Corporation, RR-1782-1-RC, 2017. As of September 24, 2021:
https://www.rand.org/pubs/research_reports/RR1782-1.html

Office of the Director of National Intelligence, *Annual Threat Assessment of the US Intelligence Community*, Washington, D.C., April 9, 2021.

Office of the Secretary of Defense, *Annual Report to Congress: Military and Security Developments Involving the People's Republic of China 2019*, Washington, D.C.: Department of Defense, May 2, 2019.

———, *Annual Report to Congress: Military and Security Developments Involving the People's Republic of China*, Washington, D.C.: Department of Defense, 2020.

———, *Annual Report to Congress: Military and Security Developments Involving the People's Republic of China 2021*, Washington, D.C.: Department of Defense, 2021.

O'Hanlon, Michael E., *The Senkaku Paradox: Risking Great Power War over Small Stakes*, Washington, D.C.: Brookings Institution Press, 2019.

Olson, Mancur, Jr., *The Economics of the Wartime Shortage: A History of British Food Supplies in the Napoleonic War and in World Wars I and II*, Durham, N.C.: Duke University Press, 1963.

O'Rourke, Ronald, *U.S.-China Strategic Competition in South and East China Seas: Background and Issues for Congress*, Washington, D.C.: Congressional Research Service, updated March 18, 2021a.

―――, *China Naval Modernization: Implications for U.S. Navy Capabilities—Background and Issues for Congress*, Washington, D.C.: Congressional Research Service, updated September 9, 2021b.

Pacific Air Forces, "US, Japan, Australia Converge on Guam for Cope North 21," February 2, 2021.

Pape, Robert A., *Bombing to Win: Air Power and Coercion in War*, Ithaca, N.Y.: Cornell University Press, 1996.

Pasandideh, Shahryar, "Do China's New Islands Allow It to Militarily Dominate the South China Sea?" *Asian Security*, Vol. 17, No. 1, 2021, pp. 1–24.

Patalano, Alessio, "When Strategy Is 'Hybrid' and Not 'Grey': Reviewing Chinese Military and Constabulary Coercion at Sea," *Pacific Review*, Vol. 31, No. 6, 2018, pp. 811–839.

Perlez, Jane, "Calls Grow in China to Press Claim for Okinawa," *New York Times*, June 13, 2013.

Porter, Patrick, "The Tyrannies of Distance: Maritime Asia and the Barriers to Conquest," in A. Trevor Thrall and Benjamin H. Friedman, eds., *US Grand Strategy in the 21st Century: The Case for Restraint*, New York: Routledge, 2018.

Posen, Barry R., "Command of the Commons: The Military Foundation of U.S. Hegemony," *International Security*, Vol. 28, No. 1, Summer 2003, pp. 5–46.

―――, *Restraint: A New Foundation for U.S. Grand Strategy*, Ithaca, N.Y.: Cornell University Press, 2014.

―――, "Europe Can Defend Itself," *Survival*, Vol. 62, No. 6, December 2020–January 2021, pp. 7–34.

Press, Daryl G., *Calculating Credibility: How Leaders Assess Military Threats*, Ithaca, N.Y.: Cornell University Press, 2005.

Priebe, Miranda, Bryan Rooney, Nathan Beauchamp-Mustafaga, Jeffrey Martini, and Stephanie Pezard, *Implementing Restraint: Changes in U.S. Regional Security Policies to Operationalize a Realist Grand Strategy of Restraint*, Santa Monica, Calif.: RAND Corporation, RR-A739-1, 2021. As of June 4, 2021:
https://www.rand.org/pubs/research_reports/RRA739-1.html

Priebe, Miranda, Alan J. Vick, Jacob L. Heim, and Meagan L. Smith, *Distributed Operations in a Contested Environment: Implications for USAF Force Presentation*, Santa Monica, Calif.: RAND Corporation, RR-2959-AF, 2019. As of February 1, 2022:
https://www.rand.org/pubs/research_reports/RR2959.html

Public Law 96-8, Taiwan Relations Act, January 1, 1979.

Quincy Institute for Responsible Statecraft, "About QI," webpage, undated. As of December 2, 2021:
https://quincyinst.org/about/

Radin, Andrew, Lynn E. Davis, Edward Geist, Eugeniu Han, Dara Massicot, Matthew Povlock, Clint Reach, Scott Boston, Samuel Charap, William Mackenzie, Katya Migacheva, Trevor Johnston, and Austin Long, *What Will Russian Military Capabilities Look Like in the Future?* Santa Monica, Calif.: RAND Corporation, RB-10038-A, 2019. As of September 20, 2021: https://www.rand.org/pubs/research_briefs/RB10038.html

Rooney, Bryan, Grant Johnson, and Miranda Priebe, *How Does Defense Spending Affect Economic Growth?* Santa Monica, Calif.: RAND Corporation, RR-A739-2, 2021. As of June 2, 2021:
https://www.rand.org/pubs/research_reports/RRA739-2.html

Rovner, Joshua, "Why Restraint in the Real World Encourages Digital Espionage," *War on the Rocks*, December 8, 2021.

Ruger, William, "To Defend America, Don't Overreach," *New York Times*, March 19, 2018.

"Ryukyu Islands," Encyclopaedia Britannica, last updated February 28, 2017. As of October 13, 2021:
https://www.britannica.com/place/Ryukyu-Islands

Sadler, Brent, "U.S. Navy," in Dakota L. Wood, ed., *2022 Index of U.S. Military Strength*, Washington, D.C.: Heritage Foundation, 2022, pp. 387–421.

Sanders, Bernie, "Ending America's Endless War: We Must Stop Giving Terrorists Exactly What They Want," *Foreign Affairs*, June 24, 2019.

Sanger, David E., "Biden Said the U.S. Would Protect Taiwan. But It's Not That Clear-Cut," *New York Times*, October 22, 2021.

Sato, Yoshimitsu, "Can the Japan Self-Defense Force Age Gracefully?" *The Diplomat*, September 18, 2019.

Schaus, John, "What Is the Philippines–United States Visiting Forces Agreement, and Why Does It Matter?" Center for Strategic and International Studies, February 12, 2020.

Schwarz, Benjamin, and Christopher Layne, "A New Grand Strategy," *The Atlantic*, January 2002.

Scobell, Andrew, "China and North Korea: Bolstering a Buffer or Hunkering Down in Northeast Asia?" testimony presented before the U.S.-China Economic and Security Review Commission on June 8, 2017, Santa Monica, Calif.: RAND Corporation, CT-477, 2017. As of February 1, 2022: https://www.rand.org/pubs/testimonies/CT477.html

Scowcroft Center for Strategy and Security, "New American Engagement Initiative," webpage, Atlantic Council, undated. As of December 1, 2021:
https://www.atlanticcouncil.org/programs/scowcroft-center-for-strategy-and-security/new-american-engagement-initiative/

Sechser, Todd S., "Goliath's Curse: Coercive Threats and Asymmetric Power," *International Organization*, Vol. 64, No. 4, Fall 2010, pp. 627–660.

Shelbourne, Mallory, "Marine Corps Ready to Conduct EABO Experiments with Allies in Indo-Pacific," USNI News, April 20, 2021.

Shifrinson, Joshua, "Should the United States Fear China's Rise?" *Washington Quarterly*, Vol. 41, No. 4, 2019, pp. 65–83.

———, "The Rise of China, Balance of Power Theory and US National Security: Reasons for Optimism?" *Journal of Strategic Studies*, Vol. 43, No. 2, 2020, pp. 175–216.

Slayton, Rebecca, "What Is the Cyber Offense-Defense Balance? Conceptions, Causes, and Assessment," *International Security*, Vol. 41, No. 3, Winter 2016–2017, pp. 72–109.

Sönnichsen, N., "Oil Consumption in China from 1998 to 2019," Statista, January 5, 2021a. As of September 7, 2021:
https://www.statista.com/statistics/265235/
oil-consumption-in-china-in-thousand-barrels-per-day/

———, "Oil Production in China from 1998 to 2019," Statista, January 5, 2021b. As of September 7, 2021:
https://www.statista.com/statistics/265196/
oil-production-in-china-since-1998-in-barrels-per-day/

Stashwick, Steven, "Japan Confirms New Missile Deployments to Ryukyu Islands," *The Diplomat*, August 6, 2021.

Stephens, Bret, Emma Ashford, and Stephen Sestanovich, "The Biden-Putin Summit: 'This Is Not About Trust,'" *New York Times*, June 16, 2021.

Sullivan, Eileen, "Trump Questions the Core of NATO: Mutual Defense, Including Montenegro," *New York Times*, July 18, 2018.

Taplin, Nathaniel, "China Is Approaching Its Own Peak Oil," *Wall Street Journal*, February 12, 2021.

Thrall, A. Trevor, and Benjamin H. Friedman, "National Interests, Grand Strategy, and the Case for Restraint," in A. Trevor Thrall and Benjamin H. Friedman, eds., *US Grand Strategy in the 21st Century: The Case for Restraint*, New York: Routledge, 2018.

Tripp, Robert S., Kristin F. Lynch, John G. Drew, and Edward W. Chan, *Supporting Air and Space Expeditionary Forces: Lessons from Operation Enduring Freedom*, Santa Monica, Calif.: RAND Corporation, MR-1819-AF, 2004. As of October 12, 2021:
https://www.rand.org/pubs/monograph_reports/MR1819.html

U.S. Census Bureau, "U.S. Trade in Goods by Country," webpage, undated. As of October 8, 2021:
https://www.census.gov/foreign-trade/balance/index.html

U.S. Department of Defense, *Indo-Pacific Strategy Report: Preparedness, Partnerships, and Promoting a Networked Region*, Arlington, Va., June 1, 2019.

U.S. Department of State, *A Free and Open Indo-Pacific: Advancing a Shared Vision*, Washington, D.C., November 4, 2019.

U.S. Forces, Japan, "Guidance from the Commander, U.S. Forces Japan," webpage, undated. As of June 16, 2021:
https://www.usfj.mil/About-USFJ/

U.S. Government Accountability Office, *Burden Sharing: Benefits and Costs Associated with the U.S. Military Presence in Japan and South Korea*, Washington, D.C., 2021.

U.S. Indo-Pacific Command, "About USINDOPACOM," webpage, undated a. As of September 24, 2021:
https://www.pacom.mil/About-USINDOPACOM/

———, "USINDOPACOM Area of Responsibility," webpage, undated b. As of September 20, 2021:
https://www.pacom.mil/About-USINDOPACOM/USPACOM-Area-of-Responsibility/

"U.S.-Japan Joint Leaders' Statement: 'U.S.–Japan Global Partnership for a New Era,'" press release, White House, April 16, 2021.

U.S. Naval Institute Staff, "USNI News Fleet and Marine Tracker: Jan. 20, 2020," *USNI News*, last updated February 10, 2020.

U.S. Navy, U.S. Marine Corps, and U.S. Coast Guard, *Advantage at Sea: Prevailing with Integrated All-Domain Naval Power*, Washington, D.C., December 2020.

Valeriano, Brandon, and Eric Gomez, "Foreign Policy Restraint: A Bold Idea for Biden's First 100 Days," *American Conservative*, January 29, 2021.

Valeriano, Brandon, and Benjamin Jensen, *The Myth of the Cyber Offense: The Case for Restraint*, Washington, D.C.: CATO Institute, Policy Analysis No. 862, January 15, 2019.

Vick, Alan J., and Mark Ashby, *Winning the Battle of the Airfields: Seventy Years of RAND Analysis on Air Base Defense and Attack*, Santa Monica, Calif.: RAND Corporation, RR-A793-1, 2021. As of December 13, 2021:
https://www.rand.org/pubs/research_reports/RRA793-1.html

Vick, Alan J., Sean M. Zeigler, Julia Brackup, and John Speed Meyers, *Air Base Defense: Rethinking Army and Air Force Roles and Functions*, Santa Monica, Calif.: RAND Corporation, RR-4368-AF, 2020. As of October 18, 2021:
https://www.rand.org/pubs/research_reports/RR4368.html

Visit Okinawa Japan, "Miyako Region," webpage, undated a. As of September 27, 2021:
https://www.visitokinawa.jp/destinations/miyako-region

———, "Yaeyama Region," webpage, undated b. As of September 27, 2021:
https://www.visitokinawa.jp/destinations/yaeyama-region

Wakim, Elee, "Sealift Is America's Achilles Heel in the Age of Great Power Competition," *War on the Rocks*, January 18, 2019.

Wallensteen, Peter, Carina Staibano, and Mikael Eriksson, *The 2004 Roundtable on UN Sanctions Against Iraq: Lessons Learned*, Uppsala, Sweden: Uppsala University, 2005.

Walt, Stephen M., *The Origins of Alliances,* Ithaca, N.Y.: Cornell University Press, 1987.

———, *Taming American Power: The Global Response to U.S. Primacy*, New York: W. W. Norton & Company, 2006.

———, "The Credibility Addiction," *Foreign Policy*, January 6, 2015.

———, *The Hell of Good Intentions: America's Foreign Policy Elite and the Decline of U.S. Primacy*, New York: Farrar, Straus and Giroux, 2018a.

———, "U.S. Grand Strategy After the Cold War: Can Realism Explain It? Should Realism Guide It?" *International Relations*, Vol. 32, No. 1, March 1, 2018b, pp. 3–22.

———, "Afghanistan Hasn't Damaged U.S. Credibility," *Foreign Policy*, August 21, 2021.

Waltz, Kenneth N., *Theory of International Politics*, Reading, Mass.: Addison-Wesley Publishing Company, Inc., 1979.

Warren, Elizabeth, "We Can End Our Endless Wars," *The Atlantic*, January 27, 2020.

Wasser, Becca, Stacie L. Pettyjohn, Jeffrey Martini, Alexandra T. Evans, Karl P. Mueller, Nathaniel Edenfield, Gabrielle Tarini, Ryan Haberman, and Jalen Zeman, *The Air War Against the Islamic State: The Role of Airpower in Operation Inherent Resolve*, Santa Monica, Calif.: RAND Corporation, RR-A388-1, 2021. As of October 7, 2021:
https://www.rand.org/pubs/research_reports/RRA388-1.html

Whalen, Jeanne, "Kim Jong Un Has a Fleet of Ghost Ships Sneaking Around the High Seas to Beat Sanctions," *Washington Post*, April 24, 2019.

White House, *National Security Strategy of the United States of America*, Washington, D.C., December 2017.

———, *Interim National Security Strategic Guidance*, Washington, D.C., March 2021.

Wong, Chun Han, "China Affirms Japan Sovereignty over Okinawa, Ryukyu Islands," *Wall Street Journal*, June 2, 2013.

Wood, Dakota L., ed., *2021 Index of U.S. Military Strength*, Washington, D.C.: Heritage Foundation, 2021.

Woolf, Amy F., *Russia's Nuclear Weapons: Doctrine, Forces, and Modernization*, Washington, D.C.: Congressional Research Service, R45861, July 2020.

Wright, Thomas, "The Case Against Restraint," interview with Elliot Waldman, *World Politics Review*, podcast, June 2, 2021.

Wuthnow, Joel, "The PLA Beyond Borders," in Joel Wuthnow, Arthur S. Ding, Phillip C. Saunders, Andrew Scobell, and Andrew N. D. Yang, eds., *The PLA Beyond Borders: Chinese Military Operations in Regional and Global Context*, Washington, D.C.: National Defense University Press, 2021, pp. 1–20.

Wuthnow, Joel, Phillip C. Saunders, and Ian Burns McCaslin, *PLA Overseas Operations in 2035: Inching Toward a Global Combat Capability*, Washington, D.C.: Institute for National Strategic Studies, National Defense University, Strategic Forum No. 309, May 2021.

Xuanzun, Liu, "China's H-6K Bomber Expected to Be Armed with Hypersonic," *Global Times*, August 6, 2019.

———, "China Conducts Mid-Course Antiballistic Missile Test, System 'Becomes More Mature, Reliable,'" *Global Times*, last updated February 5, 2021.

Yagova, Olga, "As Russia Expands Pacific Pipeline, a Third of Oil Exports Go East," Reuters, November 21, 2019.

Yeo, Mike, "Japan Names Contractor to Build Its Future Fighter Jet," Yahoo! October 30, 2020.

Yoshihara, Toshi, *Dragon Against the Sun: Chinese Views of Japanese Seapower*, Washington, D.C.: Center for Strategic and Budgetary Assessments, 2020a.

———, "How China Has Overtaken Japan in Naval Power and Why It Matters," Center for International Maritime Security, June 22, 2020b.

Yuan Yi [袁艺], "Will AI Command Future Wars?" ["人工智能将指挥未来战争?"], *Defense Daily* [中国国防报], January 12, 2017.

Zhao, Tong, *Tides of Change: U.S. Anti-Submarine Warfare and Its Impact*, Washington, D.C.: Carnegie-Tsinghua Center for Global Policy, 2018.

———, *Modernizing Without Destabilizing: China's Nuclear Posture in a New Era*, Beijing: Carnegie-Tsinghua Center for Global Policy, 2020.

Zhou, Oceana, "China's 2020 Crude Imports from US Surge 211% to 396,000 b/d, Valued at $6.28 Bil," S&P Global Platts, January 20, 2021.